# WALKS INTO HISTORY
# SUSSEX

# WALKS INTO HISTORY
# SUSSEX

## John Wilks

COUNTRYSIDE BOOKS
NEWBURY BERKSHIRE

COUNTRYSIDE BOOKS
3 Catherine Road
Newbury, Berkshire

To view our complete range of books,
please visit us at
www.countrysidebooks.co.uk

ISBN 1 85306 790 3

Designed by Graham Whiteman
Line illustrations by Trevor Yorke
Maps and photographs by the author
Cover design by Peter Davies, Nautilus Design

Typeset by Textype, Cambridge
Produced through MRM Associates Ltd, Reading
Printed by Woolnough Bookbinding Ltd., Irthlingborough

# Contents

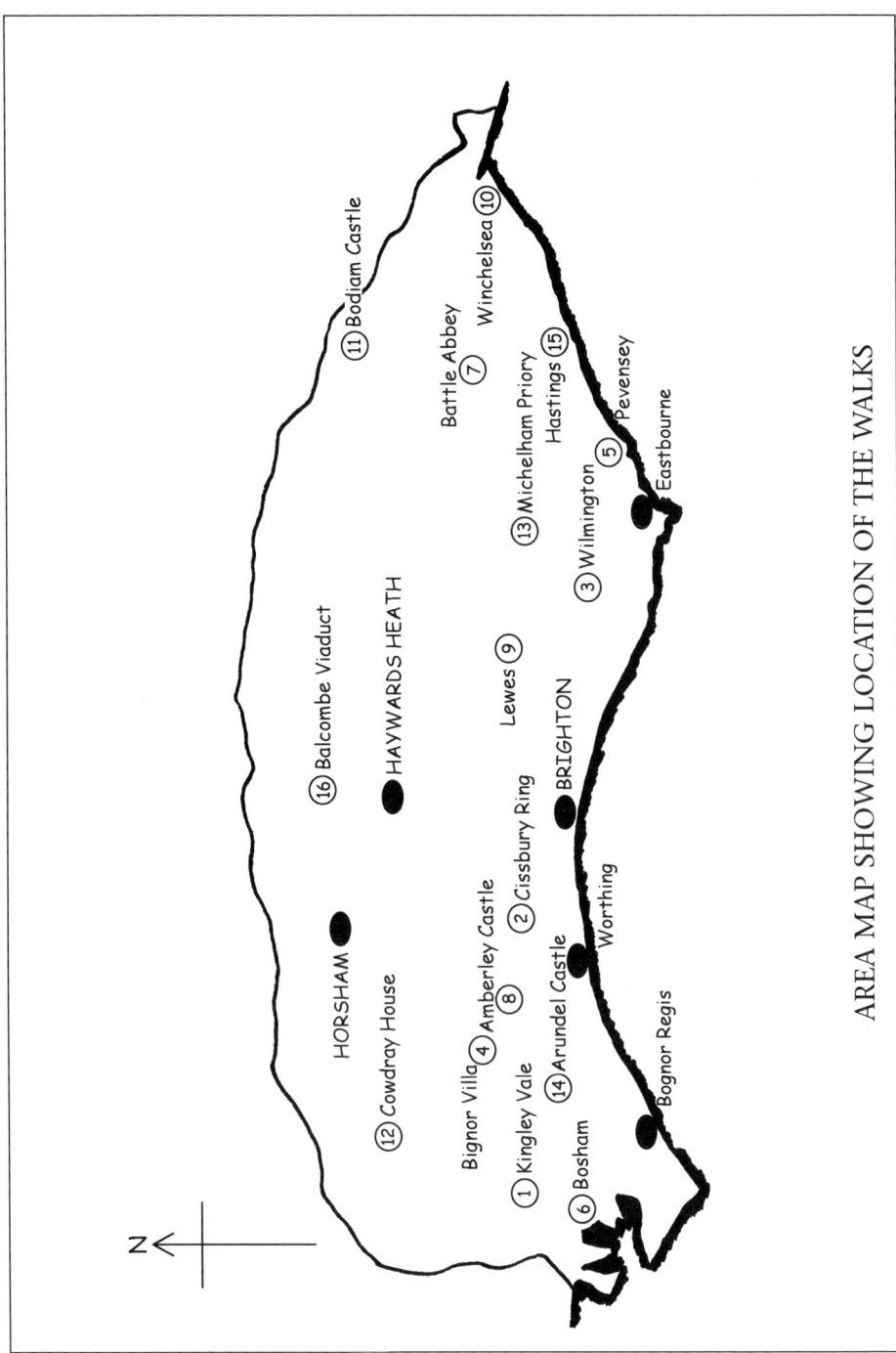

AREA MAP SHOWING LOCATION OF THE WALKS

**WALK**

**PUBLISHER'S NOTE**
We hope that you obtain considerable enjoyment from this book; great care has been taken in its preparation. Although at the time of publication all routes followed public rights of way or permitted paths, diversion orders can be made and permissions withdrawn.

We cannot, of course, be held responsible for such diversion orders and any inaccuracies in the text which result from these or any other changes to the routes nor any damage which might result from walkers trespassing on private property. We are anxious though that all details covering the walks are kept up to date and would therefore welcome information from readers which would be relevant to future editions.

The simple sketch maps that accompany the walks in this book are based on notes made by the author whilst checking out the routes on the ground. However, for the benefit of a proper map, we do recommend that you purchase the relevant Ordnance Survey sheet covering your walk. The Ordnance Survey maps are widely available, especially through booksellers and local newsagents.

# INTRODUCTION

History can be exciting and fun. Recent television series such as Simon Schama's *History of England* and *Timewatch* have proved just what an interest there is in discovering more about our past and the events that have shaped the country we know today. Sussex has always been at the heart of England's history. Its location, just across the Channel from mainland Europe, ensured that the region was almost always amongst the first to feel the reverberation and shock waves of wider political turmoil.

Today, Sussex is criss-crossed with public footpaths and they make ideal walking terrain. But, not only that, many of them pass by the sites of battlefields, invasions, Roman villas and vast, solid castles. That is why, therefore, I have chosen to write this book, *Walks Into History*.

Each circuit has been chosen because it takes the walker past sites that reveal the rich and varied history of this fascinating county. The walks are arranged chronologically and each has a major historical theme. Together they take you through 3,000 years of Sussex history. They vary in length between 3 miles and 7½ miles, but the majority are short and allow plenty of time to explore the area. All are circular, and grid references are given for the starting point. Sketch maps are included for your guidance but, for more detail, it is strongly recommended that you carry the relevant Ordnance Survey map. Convenient car parking places have been indicated for all the walks but if you do have to park on the road, please do so with consideration for other road users and take care not to block any entrances or exits. There is also a note in each chapter indicating where refreshments can be obtained but it is always advisable to have a snack with you, and more importantly a drink, especially on the longer routes. Remember also, that at certain times of the year, paths can be muddy so it is sensible to wear stout shoes.

I do hope you enjoy these walks into history and gain as much pleasure from them as I have had in devising them. Happy walking!

John Wilks

# WALK 1

# KINGLEY VALE, THE HOME OF THE DEAD

**Length: 4 miles**

*The Bronze Age tumuli at Kingley Dale*

**HOW TO GET THERE:** The walk starts from the village green in Stoughton. Stoughton is on a minor road off the B2146, north-west of Chichester and north-east of Havant.

**PARKING:** There is ample roadside parking in the village, but please park with consideration for residents.

**MAP:** OS Landranger 197 (GR 802115).

## INTRODUCTION

This pleasant walk starts in the small village of Stoughton and climbs gently to the crest of the ridge above. It then goes through an ancient and eerie forest of yews to reach Kingley Vale and the fine Bronze Age burial mounds on the open summit. From here there are great views all around, followed by a long and gradual descent back into Stoughton.

## HISTORICAL BACKGROUND

Prehistoric man lived in social groups based around an extended family, a family that included the dead as well as the living. The burial mounds at Kingley Vale were constructed as permanent homes for the dead.

Until the end of the Bronze Age, roughly 700 BC, it seems that man practised some form of ancestor worship or at least veneration. The dead were always present, in soul or spirit, and provided an on-going link between the present and the past. Selected dead were housed in huge earthen mounds, called 'barrows' or 'tumuli', constructed with a building skill that ensured they would stand for 5,000 years, the most permanent structures of their own or any other age. What ceremony was involved, or why certain individuals were chosen to be thus interred, is unknown, but it is likely that they were people who had religious rather than political importance in their lifetime. The rest of the community went into unmarked graves.

The shape and construction of barrows altered over time and from region to region. The earliest examples in Britain date from the Early Stone Age, around 4200 BC, and were 'long barrows', long cylindrical

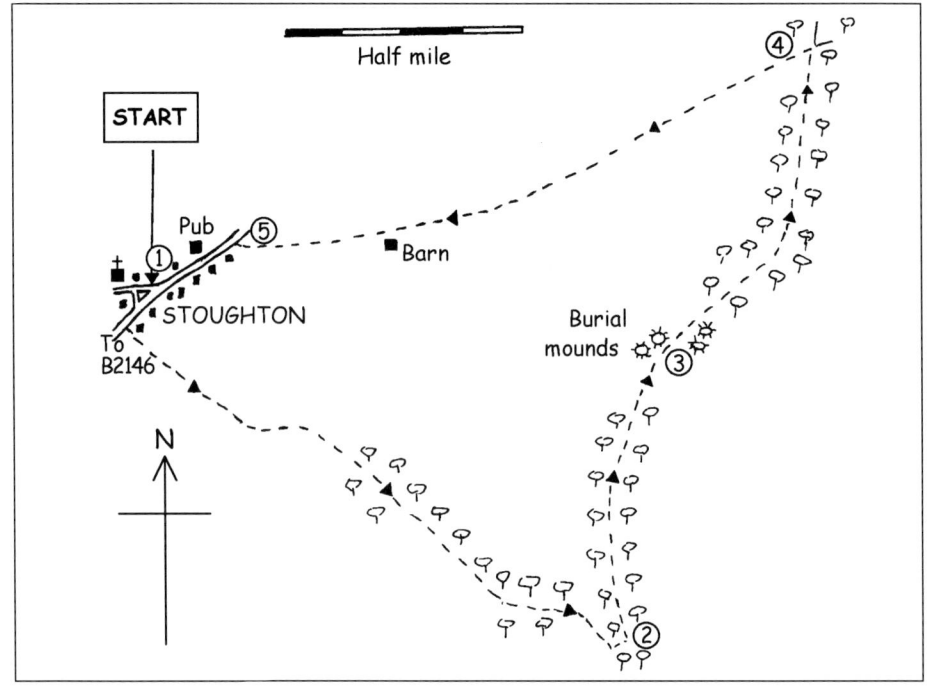

mounds in which many dead were buried, the tomb being reopened and resealed over the centuries. Later, by 3000 BC, barrows became round domes in which only a few bodies or just one body was buried.

Barrows were built upon conspicuous airy hilltops and ridges, not only for religious reasons but also for territorial ones. Each community had its own territory, and the visual presence of the tomb announced the long-term interconnection between a group of people and a specific area of land. Before the woods grew up which obscure today's skyline, the barrows above Kingley Vale would have been visible for miles.

## THE WALK

❶ Walk along the village street back towards the B2146, with the village green on your right, passing the drive to St Mary's church.

*This late Saxon church was built in 1050, just before the Norman Conquest.*

At the end of a flint walled farm on your left, turn left up a drive, with Tythe Barn House on the right. Climb gently up a grassy track, then continue as it becomes steeper and curves left, eventually passing into trees. At the top of the slope, emerge from the woods and keep ahead on a grassy track with a fence to your right. Follow the right-hand fence, ignoring two bridleways going off to the left. About 100 yards after the second bridleway, where the fence turns right, keep straight on into the woods.

*This is one of the largest yew forests in Europe. The huge gnarled trees grow so closely together that they blot out the light, and consequently nothing else flourishes. Some of the trees here are over 500 years old and the forest itself dates back at least 1,300 years.*

A path joins from the right. Keep straight on, descending through the yews.

*Soon there are views down to the coast, over Chichester and Bosham. In the Bronze Age these slopes were not forested, and the vista would have been far more open.*

On reaching a cross-track in an open grassy area, cross to a stile in the fence half-right ahead. Cross the stile and go half-right on a path, initially parallel to the track on your right beyond the fence, but soon diverging. Follow the path for 100 yards to a cross-path at a post.

❷   Turn left and follow the path uphill through yews for ½ a mile to emerge at a stile. Cross the stile and go half-left up the slope to the tumuli.

*The round barrows here are a specific design known as 'bell tumuli', so called because they were constructed in a bell shape. They were built around 700 BC and are among the last tumuli constructed in Britain. After that date, different forms of burial were adopted. There are relatively few bell tumuli in Britain, and these are some of the finest examples. It would have taken about 10,000 man-hours to construct just one. The whole community would have worked together to build the barrow, which could have been done in a few months when time became available after the harvest was in.*

*Burial practices altered considerably over the millennia when barrows were in use. The earlier long barrows were communal graves, reused over a long period, and initially bodies would have been left exposed to the air and scavengers until only scattered bones remained to be buried. Later bodies were cremated and the ashes interred. The two tumuli here were*

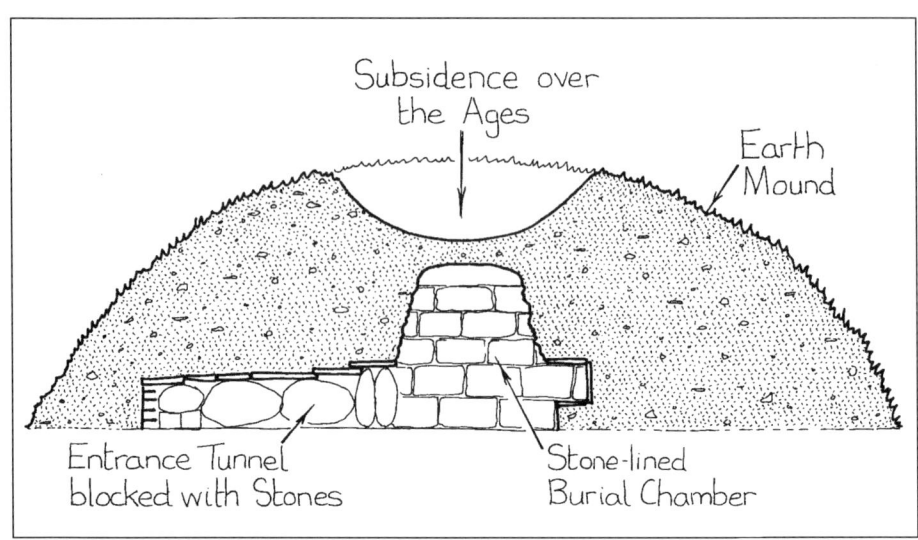

*A cross-section of a bell tumulus*

*each used as the grave of one individual only, and the bodies were buried intact, but crouched up into a foetal position.*

**REFRESHMENTS**

The Hare and Hounds in Stoughton is a small country pub with a beer garden. It is open all day (telephone: 01705 631433).

*Even today, there are fine views from here, right down to the coast to the south, and northwards to the Downs. In turn, the barrows can be seen for miles.*

❸   To continue the walk pass the tumuli on your left. Just after the second tumulus, bear left on a grassy path to a signboard and a chalky track beyond. Turn right along the chalk track.

*There are two more tumuli on your right.*

Ignore two footpaths climbing to the right but continue on the track, descending slightly to eventually emerge from the woods.

❹   At a junction of paths, with a fingerpost off to the left, turn left on a path, with a fence on your left and trees on your right. Descend the path, soon enclosed, with Stoughton seen in the valley ahead. The path joins a track. Continue straight on to the farm buildings below, ignoring side turns. Pass the farm buildings on your left and continue down the track. At a barn bear right with the track to reach a lane.

❺   Turn left and follow the lane back into Stoughton.

# Walk 2

# Cissbury Ring and the First Arms Race

**Length: 3½ or 4½ miles**

*Cissbury hill fort*

**HOW TO GET THERE:** The walk starts from the Village House public house, at the crossroads in the centre of Findon village. Findon is ½ mile to the east of the A24, and 3 miles north of Worthing.

**PARKING:** There is ample roadside parking in the village, but please park with consideration for the residents.

**MAP:** OS Landranger 198 (GR 123088).

## Introduction

This short but exhilarating walk climbs out of the village of Findon and soon follows an ancient trackway across the top of the Downs, with fine views to both sides and with Cissbury Ring dominating the landscape. On Cissbury Ring, the best preserved hill fort in Sussex, there is the opportunity to walk right around the ramparts, with wonderful airy views on all sides, before returning on field paths to Findon.

## HISTORICAL BACKGROUND

From 1000 BC onwards the climate across the British Isles deteriorated, becoming colder and wetter. The rising water-table made the soil of the Downs too heavy and wet for growing crops, whilst the traditionally settled land in the river valleys was becoming exhausted as, after centuries of intensive farming, the soil deteriorated. At the same time the population had increased dramatically, both in the upland and lowland areas, and competition for the available arable land greatly intensified.

This demand for land coincided with a greater use of iron for tools and for weapons. Iron was easier to work than bronze, and iron ore was much more readily available. Consequently, there was a proliferation of iron weapons and they were soon used to settle the ever more frequent conflicts over land. For protection, families and tribes gathered into loose confederations and petty kingdoms, headed by a ruling elite versed in the ways of war.

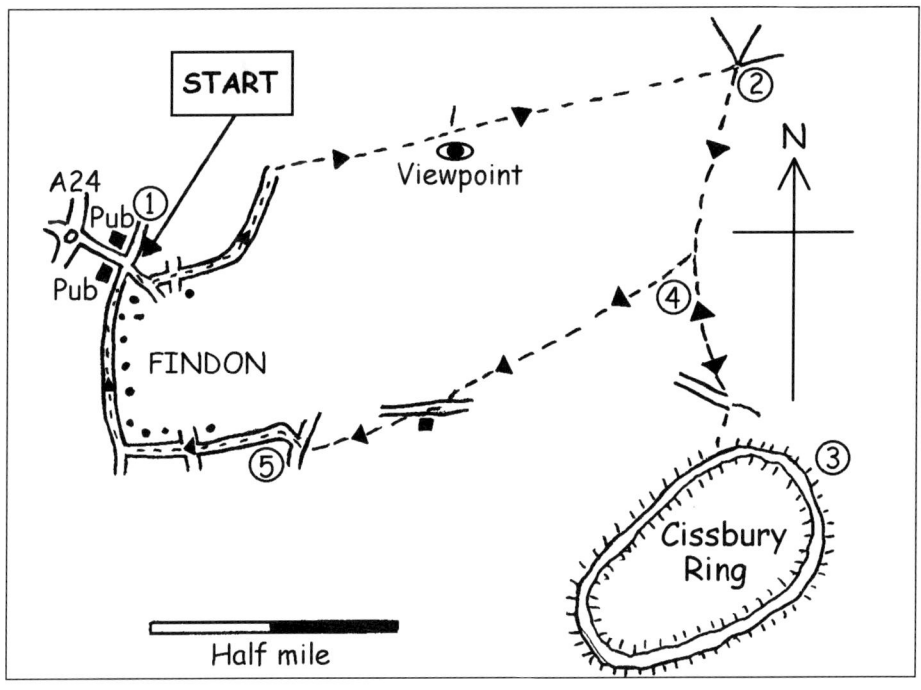

Inter-tribal warfare was by no means endemic, and by and large these groups co-existed peacefully. However, the threat of violence was always there, and to counter this there was a need for a tribe to have a defensive site to which the population could withdraw in times of emergency. Communities increasingly lived in the shadow of hill forts, which could offer protection. These forts in turn were built ever larger and grander, a visible symbol of the power and prestige of the local ruler.

The most splendid hill fort in Sussex is Cissbury Ring. With its huge ramparts and dominating position, it was clearly designed to overawe potential enemies. Like the modern day nuclear deterrent the important thing about hill forts in the Iron Age was their existence, not their use, for no tribal army of that day could reasonably hope to take such an impregnable obstacle by force.

### THE WALK

❶    With your back to the two pubs, walk along the road opposite, The Square. In 40 yards turn left, signed 'Cissbury Ring, unsuitable for motor vehicles'. Climb with the lane and at the top of the slope bear left with the road. At the entrance to Gallops Farm turn right along the track.

*This track follows the line of an ancient Iron Age trading route, following the crest of the Downs and running from the natural harbours of the Solent to the Kent coast. Cissbury Ring was built close by, providing protection for passing traders and a visible symbol of the strength of its builders.*

Follow the track. Ignore a footpath in 250 yards, but in a further 200 yards, where a footpath crosses the track, look right, to Cissbury Ring dominating the skyline.

*The huge bulk of Cissbury Ring covers the whole of the hilltop opposite. Indeed, it is so vast that at first glance it appears a natural feature and not man-made at all. In Iron Age times the ramparts would have been steeper, not softened as now by two millennia of erosion, and topped by high, strong walls. The sight must have been truly awesome to Iron Age man, a visible impression of unassailable power.*

Continue on the track along the crest of the Downs for a further ½ mile to reach a junction of tracks, where the fence on the right turns a corner.

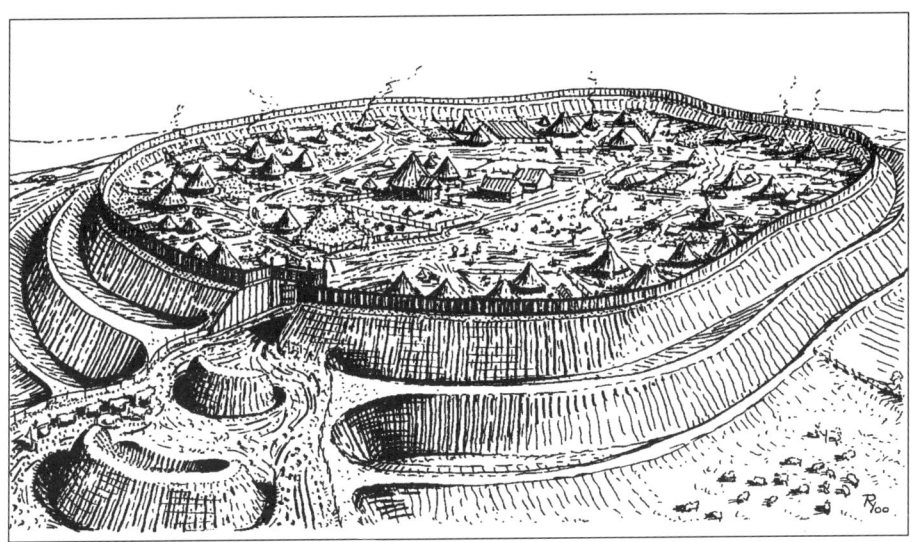

*Artist's impression of Cissbury Ring*

❷ Turn right with the fence and follow the track towards Cissbury Ring, ignoring a footpath off to the side. Cross a parking area at the head of a minor road and go straight on through a kissing gate and onto Cissbury Ring. Climb the steps through the ramparts to the summit of the fort.

*Cissbury Ring was built around 250 BC. A double rampart, with ditches on the outer side of each, cut off a spur of the Downs and enclosed a site 30 hectares in area. Originally, the banks would have been far more precipitous than today, and topped with a strong wooden palisade for added protection.*

*In times of peace, the hill fort was an administrative and commercial centre for the tribe, with huts for the regular inhabitants, stockades and temporary accommodation for passing traders. The rest of the tribe would have lived in outlying farms, on the surrounding Downs and in the valley below. In times of war, the fort would have provided emergency shelter for the whole community, and in the centre there was plenty of open space to house the cattle of the surrounding farms.*

*Cissbury Ring would have been virtually impregnable against attack by neighbouring tribes, who lacked the weapons – or the discipline – to storm its ramparts. There is no sign that the Ring was ever attacked, its deterrent effect being enough to ensure that peaceful relations with its neighbours were maintained.*

Turn left along the upper rampart
and walk as far as the eastern
gate.

*On three sides the natural slope of
the land drops away sharply to the
valley below and provides increased
protection. Only on the northern*
side, which you are now walking along, was there access across relatively
flat land, and here the ramparts were built with extra height and strength.

> **REFRESHMENTS**
>
> The Village House is a spacious historic pub
> with lots of racing memorabilia. It offers a
> wide range of food and a changing variety of
> beers (telephone: 01903 873350). There is also
> a village store in Findon.

❸   At the eastern gate you can either return to the entrance steps
along the lower rampart, or continue the full circuit of the upper
rampart, a further ¾ mile.

*There were originally two gates into Cissbury Ring. This one, on the eastern
side of the fort, gave access to the ridge and to the major trade route that
ran along the top of the Downs. A second gate, on the southern side of the
fort, led to the valley below, where the bulk of the tribe lived on scattered
farms.*

*The gate was always the weakest point of a hill fort's defences, and was
protected by extra ramparts, the outline of which can just be made out. The
gate itself would have been a movable wooden structure, often a pile of
sturdy logs.*

After viewing Cissbury Ring descend by the entrance steps back to
the parking area. Keep straight on along the track for 400 yards, and
then turn left into an enclosed footpath.

❹   Follow the footpath for ½ mile to reach a lane. Turn right down
the lane for 100 yards, until just beyond a house on the left, and
then turn left through wooden barriers onto a small common. Walk
diagonally across the common towards the houses opposite. Follow
the grassy track along the front of the houses to reach a road.

❺   Cross the road and go along Steep Lane opposite. At a crossroads
keep ahead down the lane to reach the main road through Findon.
Turn right and along the village high street back to the start, passing
the East Lodge of Findon Park en route.

# A WALK WITH THE CELTIC GODS: THE LONG MAN OF WILMINGTON

**Length: 6 miles**

*The Long Man of Wilmington*

**HOW TO GET THERE:** Alfriston is 2 miles south of the A27 on the B2108, midway between Lewes and Eastbourne. The walk starts from the Star Inn in Alfriston High Street.

**PARKING:** There are two pay-and-display car parks on the northern outskirts of the village, only a few minutes walk along the High Street from the Star.

**MAP:** OS Landranger 199 (GR 521033).

## INTRODUCTION

This walk starts from the beautiful village of Alfriston with a delightful stroll beside the Cuckmere River. It then climbs gently for a spectacular and airy stretch along the South Downs, before reaching the Long Man of Wilmington, one of the largest and most mysterious chalk figures on the Downs. The route returns through Wilmington, with its old church and yew tree, and across fields back to Alfriston. The walking and route-finding are easy throughout. There is one gentle ascent and descent.

## HISTORICAL BACKGROUND

In pre-Roman times, the race known as the Celts occupied a vast territory, stretching from Ireland to the Black Sea. Today their culture and language survive only on the fringes of Europe. Across England only occasional monuments to the Celts survive, of which the Long Man of Wilmington is one of the most mysterious and evocative.

The so-called 'Ancient Britons' were part of this far-flung Celtic world. Celtic society was tribal. Extended families lived together under a chieftain, smaller tribal units would join together into larger confederations, who were often at war with one another. The society was also very hierarchical. At the top were a king and nobles, who provided the warrior class necessary to defend the tribe, and also the master craftsmen, the doctors, the specialist workmen and the men of learning, the bards and the priests. Below them were freemen, the peasant farmers and the less skilled workmen, and at the bottom of the pyramid were the slaves.

The enemies of the Celts, the Greeks and later the Romans, portrayed them as war-crazed, woad-painted barbarians, whose only interests were fighting and orgies, but the reality is very different. The Celts were an energetic race who created brilliant and vibrant art, poetry and music, and had complex and deeply thought-out religious beliefs. They lived in settled communities, often quite large towns, and produced sophisticated and ingenious iron tools. What

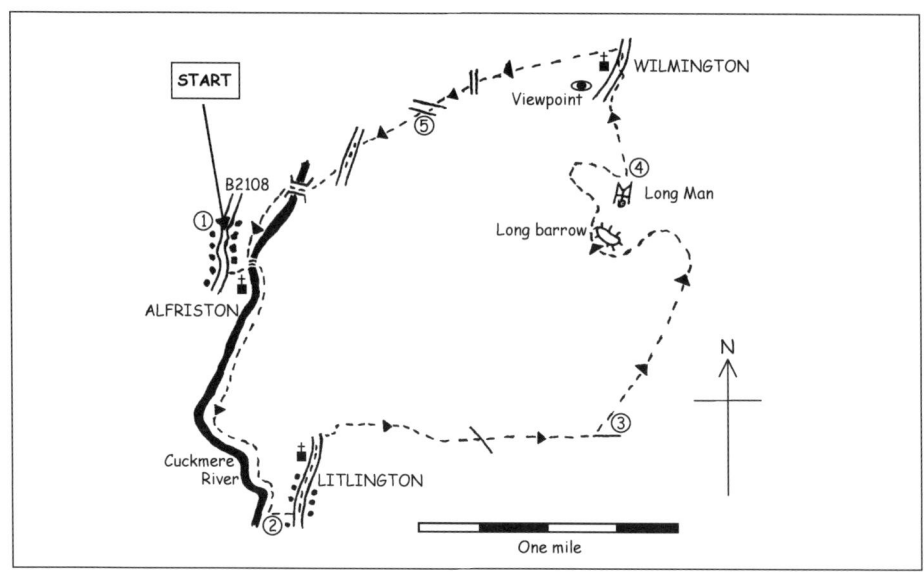

the Celts did not have was a written language, and the image of them that has survived is the written propaganda of their conquerors.

The Celts were a race of warrior-farmers, and the basis of Celtic life was the land. Their religion reflects this. They did not believe in one god but in a host of deities, many of whom reflected aspects of nature. Celtic religious art had many representations of their gods. Some, carved in wood or stone, were tiny and intricate. Others, carved into the land itself, were huge, and the largest of all can be seen at Wilmington.

## THE WALK

❶   With your back to the Star Inn, cross the road to the George Inn and turn right along the High Street. In 30 yards turn left down an alley. Do not turn right to the church and the Clergy House, but instead continue ahead along an enclosed alley, passing the Memorial Hall on your right. Continue ahead across the footbridge. At the far end turn right through a kissing gate onto the river bank. Continue with the river on your right for ¾ mile, then 50 yards before a footbridge, turn left along a tarmac path.

❷   Follow the enclosed footpath out to a road and turn left through the village of Litlington, eventually passing the church on your left. Some 50 yards past the church, turn right up a farm drive (signed 'Public Bridleway'). After 30 yards, turn left and follow the signed track past cowsheds. Follow the track as it bears right and climbs. After ½ mile keep straight on over a cross-track, but in another 600 yards, bear left at a fork.

❸   Follow the clear track across the side of the hill, a deep dry valley off to your left. Where the track turns right at the end of the first large field, keep ahead through a gate and maintain your direction across the down, with a fence and gorse on your left. Follow the path as it curves left around the head of the dry valley to join a track. Maintain your direction, now on a chalky track. Keep ahead through a gate (ignoring stiles to your right) and continue ahead along the spur, aiming at the prominent long barrow seen ahead.

*This is Windhover long barrow, 60 yards long and 17 wide, the largest burial mound in Sussex. It was dug 3,500 years ago, during the Bronze Age. An avenue or 'cursus', almost indistinguishable now, led from the barrow, in the general direction of the Long Man of Wilmington on the slope below. In Bronze Age religious beliefs, the barrow was the resting place of the body, while the cursus was the road leading the spirit to the afterlife. Although it is sometimes claimed that the Long Man is part of this complex, the carving was not made until 1,500 years after the long barrow and cursus.*

Pass the long barrow on your right and follow the track as it descends and curves to the right. Descend with the track around the side of another dry valley, with views of Alfriston off to your left. When the track meets a fence on the right, DO NOT bear left with the main track to a gate, but instead bear slightly right and descend with a track, the fence close on your right. In 200 yards turn right through a gate. Follow the path along the side of the hill, with a fence on your left hand, soon reaching the foot of the Long Man of Wilmington.

*The Long Man of Wilmington is 231 ft tall, and is claimed to be the largest representation of the human form in the world. Today it is outlined in white paint, replacing white bricks put in by Victorian restorers. Whether the figure was originally outlined with stones or simply cut into the chalk is unknown.*

*The Long Man is in a shallow natural amphitheatre in the chalk ridge, which conceals the figure when approached from certain angles. It is unique amongst hill figures in England in holding two staves in its hands. Unlike other hill figures, it is not sexually explicit. This appears to have been the original design and not the result of modesty by later restorers.*

*The origins of the Long Man are uncertain. It was originally assumed that it was Bronze Age, and thus part of the Windhover long barrow complex on the hill above. A later theory attributed the figure to the Romans – an image of the Emperor Constantine designed to impress the local population. Another theory claims the figure represents Odin, warrior-god of the Vikings. Since there is no written mention of the figure before the 19th century it is impossible to date it with precision, but the most plausible explanation is that it is Celtic in origin, 2,000 years old or so, dating from the years before the Roman invasion.*

*One of the most important deities of the Ancient Britons, or Celts, was Lugh (or Lugus), a god of the harvest. Lugh protected cattle and crops, ensured that the seasons came and went in their proper course, and represented balance and harmony in nature. He is often depicted holding measuring rods, to represent his skills as a judge and mediator. To a society whose lives were closely tied to the land, a god such as Lugh was immensely important, and it is likely that the Long Man was carved as a sign of devotion and as a plea for divine protection.*

❹ From the foot of the Long Man, go through a gate on the left and follow a clear track down between fields towards the road. Just before the road, turn right through a squeeze stile and follow the path alongside the road. Emerge in Wilmington village opposite a parking area with toilets.

*From the picnic area adjoining the car park there is the best view of the Long Man.*

Turn right along the road for 100 yards, passing the entrance to the Priory, and then turn left into the churchyard.

*Wilmington Priory was founded in 1088 by William the Conqueror's half-brother Robert de Mortain. It was a very minor Benedictine religious house, and had decayed long before the Dissolution of the Monasteries, becoming a farmhouse. The adjoining church of St Mary and St Peter was built to serve the Priory, and replaced an earlier wooden Saxon chapel.*

*The ancient yew in Wilmington Churchyard*

*However, there is evidence in the churchyard that suggests this may have been a site of worship even before the Saxon building – a huge and wonderful yew tree, dating back to AD 390 and thus being over 1,600 years old. The yew had great religious significance in pre-Christian Celtic Britain. Deities were to be found in forests and groves, marshes, lakes, rivers and springs. Druids, religious leaders of great importance, conducted services in groves. The yew has dark red berries fruiting at the time of Midwinter's Day, a time when the world is at its coldest and darkest, and thus was important in ceremonies based around renewing the Earth and calling the sun back. Yew trees and their berries became incorporated into the later Christian symbols of Christmas.*

> **REFRESHMENTS**
>
> The Star Inn is a fascinating old building that dates from the 15th century, and was a resthouse for pilgrims going to the shrine of St Richard in Chichester. It offers a wide range of food and beers (telephone: 01904 620033). Additionally, there are several other pubs, as well as tearooms and shops, in Alfriston.

*Nature worship was part of Celtic belief, and the yew tree and the Long Man are both part of this. In an attempt to suppress pagan religions, the Christians often built chapels on pagan sites. It is not too fanciful to assume the yew tree here, which pre-dates the Saxon chapel and the later Norman church, was used as a site of pagan nature worship.*

Bear right through the churchyard and exit by a gate. Cross the lane and keep ahead across two fields. DO NOT follow the track into the farm at the end of the second field but instead cross a stile to the left of the farm. Keep ahead to a stile leading into a lane. Cross the lane and the stile opposite, and keep ahead across the field beyond. Follow the waymarked path past a paddock, and then diagonally across the next field to a lane beyond.

❺   Cross the stile opposite and follow the clear path across the field beyond. At the end of the field, go half-right to a stile leading into a lane, the ragstone-faced Milton Court immediately opposite. Turn left along the lane for 150 yards. At the end of Milton Court Farm, turn right through a kissing gate then go diagonally right across the next two fields to reach the road at a bridge. Turn right across the bridge then immediately turn left through a gate onto the riverbank. Follow the river back into Alfriston.

# WALK 4
# BIGNOR VILLA, AND THE ARRIVAL OF THE ROMANS

**Length: 5 miles**

*Bignor Roman Villa*

**HOW TO GET THERE:** Bignor lies 2 miles to the west of the A29 at Bury.

**PARKING:** The walk starts from a free car park on the summit of the South Downs. The car park is clearly signed from Bignor village.

**MAP:** OS Landranger 197 (GR 973129).

## INTRODUCTION

This walk starts on the crest of the South Downs, and descends through woodland to visit Bignor, with its magnificent Roman villa and interesting medieval church. It then continues across rolling farmland, with fine views, before climbing steeply through woods to return along the crest of the Downs.

## HISTORICAL BACKGROUND

The area of modern-day Sussex rapidly grew in prosperity after the Romans arrived, and there are few finer examples of this prosperity than the villa at Bignor.

In AD 43 Sussex was the territory of the Regnenses, a confederation of small Iron Age kingdoms whose wealth was based upon the rich agricultural land north of the Downs. The initial war aim of the Roman invasion was the defeat of the hostile tribes of Kent and Essex. These tribes were long-time enemies of the Regnenses, who took no part in opposing the invasion and rapidly became a client state of the Romans. By AD 47, a mere four years after the first legions landed in Kent, the Romans occupied all of south-east Britain, with a frontier running from the Wash to the Bristol Channel, and set about consolidating their conquest.

The Romans had no prejudice against race or colour and easily assimilated new populations, and part of their genius was in getting local inhabitants to accept the material benefits of Roman civilisation and thus to have a stake in preserving the Empire. West Sussex was already an important agricultural area, especially for the

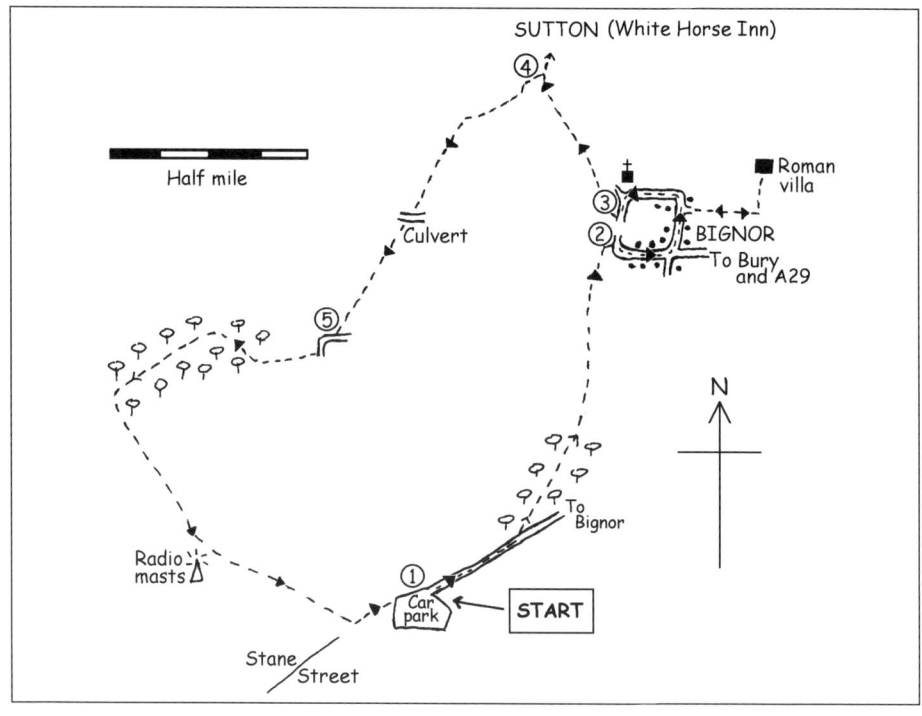

raising of sheep, and the Romans set about developing it still further, partly by introducing new methods of production and partly by providing access to a huge and stable market. At one level peasant settlements, villages and simple farmsteads, continued to function much as they had done before the invasion, but superimposed upon these were new communities based upon villas. An elaborate house was generally the administrative centre of a large farm. It was surrounded by outbuildings such as barns and stables and the dwellings of farm workers, and was in the centre of orchards and fields. The villas were built close to the Roman roads, which gave access to markets, and they were the hub of Roman-style agriculture in Sussex. They were usually owned, not by foreigners, but by native Britons who had seen the benefits of the Roman system and had embraced the Roman way of life.

## THE WALK

❶  From the car park, walk down the access road back towards Bignor.

*This access road follows the course of Stane Street, the old Roman road that connected Noviomagus Regnensium, modern Chichester, with London. Noviomagus Regnensium had been the capital of the Regnenses and the Romans made it into their major administrative centre on the south coast. A prosperous city and port soon grew up, facing the vast Roman Empire across the Channel. Stane Street was a major trade route linking London and Britain to the Continent. Bignor Villa was only a few hundred yards from Stane Street, connected to it by a metalled track, and its prosperity owed much to its ready access to the main road.*

Follow the lane for 600 yards and then turn left at a fingerpost. Follow the footpath down through woods. At the bottom of the slope go over a cross-track and continue ahead on an enclosed footpath, with a field to your left. At the end of the enclosed footpath cross a stile and keep ahead, with a hedge on your right. Continue to a waymark post in the field corner. Cross a stile and continue for 5 yards to a cross-track. Turn right and follow the track and stream to a lane.

❷  **If you do not wish to visit Bignor Roman villa or the village,** turn left for 100 yards, passing a row of cottages. At the far end of a small field turn left through a gate and continue from point 3.

**To visit the villa or the village, with its interesting medieval church**, turn right along the lane and follow it around a left-hand corner to a junction. Ignore a right turn but instead turn left, signed 'Sutton, Duncton'. Continue along the road for 100 yards to a side road on the right, signed 'no through road'. For the villa, turn right along this side road, and where it ends keep ahead along a field track for 300 yards to reach the entrance. Bignor Roman Villa is open daily from 1st March to 31st October, 10 am to 5 pm (6 pm from June to September). It is privately owned and there is an admission charge (telephone: 01798 869259).

*This rich agricultural land had been cultivated before the Romans arrived, and where the present villa now stands were the fields of the Iron Age farmers. The first settlement here during the Roman era was a farmstead surrounded by a ditched enclosure, built around the end of the 1st century AD, some 50 years after the Roman occupation of the area. Whilst the farm produced food for its own needs, with a surplus for local sale, it mainly concentrated upon sheep farming. The sheep grazed the Downs, whilst the farm was the centre of a woollen industry, where the sheep were sheared and their wool cleaned, woven and dyed.*

*With the growing demands from Roman Britain this farmstead steadily increased in prosperity. A substantial timber manor house was erected around AD 190-200, replaced by a stone-built house 50 years later. This steadily grew over the years, as the owners became wealthier. At its peak Bignor Villa had over 50 rooms, grouped around a large courtyard and with a huge walled enclosure adjoining.  Bignor became one of the most luxurious villas in Britain, with elaborate baths, underfloor heating, and richly decorated corridors that allowed for indoor promenades when the weather was bad. It is especially famous for its floor mosaics, among the finest ever found in England, with a high and costly level of craftsmanship which speaks eloquently of the wealth of Bignor's owners.*

*It must be remembered that these owners were not foreigners but were native British who had embraced the Roman way of life, and grown rich within the Roman Empire. It seems likely that one extended family owned Bignor throughout the Roman period.*

After viewing the villa, retrace your steps to the entrance of the no through road, where you turn right and follow the lane around a left-hand bend. Some 200 yards later, opposite the church gate, turn left

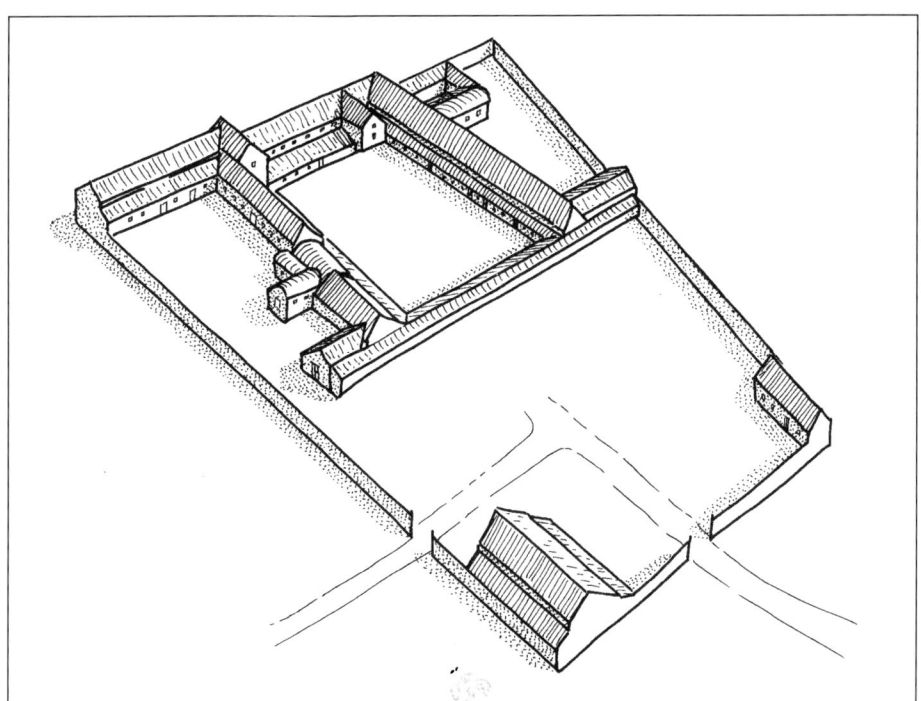

*Bignor Villa in the 4th century*

down the lane for 150 yards. At the end of 'Charmans', turn right through a gate.

❸   Once through the gate continue ahead, passing a house and bank close on your right. Follow the path down into trees and over a footbridge, then continue through woods to another footbridge at the end of the pond. Walk along the clear path to a stile, then cross the field beyond to a gap in the hedge and climb to a stile on the skyline. Continue on a clear track across the next field to a waymark post.

❹   **To visit the White Horse Inn at Sutton**, continue along the enclosed footpath ahead for a few yards.

To continue the walk, turn left at the waymark post (right if coming from Sutton) and follow the field boundary, with the hedge on your right, to reach a stile. Cross the next field to another stile and then carry on along the edge of a third field, with the hedge again on your right, passing the end of a street on your right. Where the hedge ends keep straight on along a clear path across a field to a stile, aiming directly at masts seen on the skyline. Cross the stile and

descend through trees. At the foot of the slope, maintain the same direction across a grassy strip to a fingerpost, then turn left over a culvert. Cross the next field to a stile in the top right-hand corner (still aiming at the masts). Cross this stile and continue in the same direction across the next field, still aiming at the masts and at houses opposite, to reach a lane.

❺   Turn right along the lane for 100 yards. Turn left with the lane around a corner and immediately bear right to a fingerpost at a field entrance. Go half-right across the field, then swing right with the clear path to cross a second field and enter woods. Bear left with the footpath and climb steeply through the trees to reach a cross-track, where you turn left. The gradient is now gentler. Follow the track to a junction at a fingerpost near the summit of the hill. Continue ahead, avoiding turns to left and right. In 10 yards bear left with the track to emerge from the wood. Follow the track along the summit of the Downs. At a 'NT Bignor Hill' sign, ignore a track to the right but continue ahead along the track you are on, soon passing the radio masts on your right. You soon have excellent views all around of the Weald, the Downs and the coast. At a cross-track turn left, joining Stane Street just before you reach the car park.

*All Roman roads were built to the same design. The road surface was raised and 'metalled', with layers of pounded flint and chalk, and a ditch was dug on both sides for drainage. To either side of the road was a flat open area from which all vegetation and obstructions had been cleared, to remove any danger of ambush. There is a remarkably well-preserved section of Stane Street a mile to the south-west of the car park.*

# WALK 5
# TWO CASTLES AND TWO INVASIONS, THE STORY OF PEVENSEY

**Length: 5 miles**

*The Norman castle of Pevensey*

**HOW TO GET THERE:**
Pevensey itself lies on the A259, midway between Hastings and Eastbourne.

**PARKING:** The walk starts from the Old Cattle Market pay-and-display car park next to Pevensey Castle.

**MAP:** OS Landranger 199 (GR 648049).

## INTRODUCTION

This walk starts at Pevensey Castle, and then crosses Pevensey Levels, following the route taken by William the Conqueror along the banks of Pevensey Haven. The return is across fields. The Levels, although flat, are very scenic and full of interest, and have a remote feel that belies their closeness to Pevensey.

## HISTORICAL BACKGROUND

The first castle at Pevensey was built towards the end of the Roman occupation, one of the so-called 'Forts of the Saxon Shore' built to defend Britain against raiders from across the North Sea.

By the 5th century AD the Roman Empire was under threat on all sides, as barbarian tribes pushed against the frontiers. The province of Britain was increasingly threatened in the north and west by its old enemies, the Picts and the Scots, but to these were added a new and greater danger from the south, the Saxons. Crossing the North Sea from present day Germany and Holland, the Saxons raided the exposed coast of Britain. To counter this, a string of forts were built from the Wash to the Solent. Pevensey was one of the largest and most modern of these.

In Roman times the sea came right up to where Pevensey Castle now stands. The coastline was wild, bleak and marshy, uninhabited

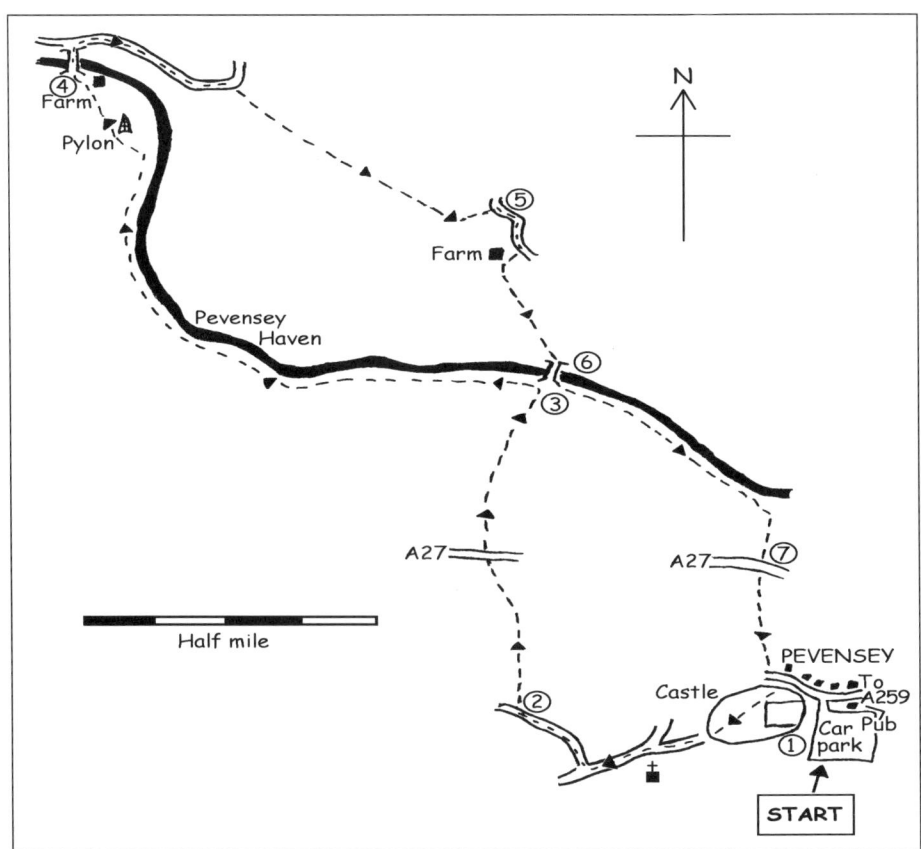

until the Romans built their fort. A town and port, called Anderida, soon grew up around the fort. After the Romans withdrew from Britain in AD 410, Saxon raids grew ever more frequent and violent, with settlement instead of mere plunder increasingly the aim. The Romano-British inhabitants continued to use the fort of Pevensey as part of their attempt to hold back the Saxons, but in AD 491 it fell after a six month siege to the Saxon warchief Aelle, who, in retribution for holding out so long, slaughtered all the inhabitants. This massacre ended any real opposition to the Saxons. Over the next decades Saxon settlers poured into the area, which became known as the land of the 'South Saxons', or 'Sussex'.

In 1066 William the Conqueror crossed the Channel to invade England (see Walk 7). Rather than land at the defended port of Hastings, William chose to land his invasion fleet at Pevensey, with its sheltered anchorage and its now ruined and undefended fort, before marching inland to attack Hastings from the rear. After the throne of England was securely his, William made sure that no future foreign invader could use it as a landing point. He gave it to one of his supporters, who built the strong Norman castle seen today.

## THE WALK
❶ From the car park entrance turn left through the gates of Pevensey Castle.

*In Roman times the sea came right up to the walls of the castle. The car park would have been the sea and the road the side of the harbour. The castle was built on a peninsula, connected to the land on the far side of the castle, with marshes to the west, the harbour to the north and the sea to the south and east.*

Go through a kissing gate and follow a surfaced path through the fort.

*The huge open space in front of you and to your right was the old Roman fort. Built in AD 340, it was one of nine 'Forts of the Saxon Shore', and whereas in most cases existing forts were strengthened and regarrisoned, the building at Pevensey was new. As the only purpose-built Saxon Shore fort, it represented state-of-the-art military architecture. The walls were taller than normal and extra thick, and followed the irregular outline of the peninsula they surrounded, rather than being built in the normal Roman square or rectangular shape. The walls enclosed ten acres, and the settlement that grew into the Roman town of Anderida started off within them. The garrison was not one of the crack Roman legions (which were normally manned by foreigners) but an auxiliary unit known as a 'numerus', many of whose members would have been recruited from the local population.*

Turn slightly left to view the Norman castle. From April until the end of September it is open 10 am to 6 pm; in October from 10 am until dusk; November to March 10 am until 4 pm. Admission charge; free to members of English Heritage.

*The castle you see before you is a thousand years younger than the Roman fort in which it stands. The first Norman castle was built here in 1067, the year after the Conquest. William the Conqueror gave lands to his trusted supporters, partly as a reward but also so that they could control his conquered kingdom for him. Pevensey was given to William's half-brother Robert de Mortain, who immediately built a wood and earth castle in the corner of the old Roman ruins, whose walls, although tumbled down, gave some added protection. By 1100 the present stone-walled keep, with five towers and a surrounding moat, was built, and the old Roman walls were refortified to create a huge outer bailey.*

*Pevensey Castle, with its important strategic location, saw action on a number of occasions. In 1087 William the Conqueror died and the throne was disputed between his two sons. Pevensey was held by another of William's half-brothers, Bishop Odo, who was besieged here the following year by one of the contenders for the throne, William Rufus. Starvation finally forced Odo's surrender. In 1147 the castle was again starved into surrender, when it supported Queen Matilda's claims to the throne and was besieged by her cousin, King Stephen.*

*In the 14th century it was besieged twice. In 1264, supporters of King Henry III fled to Pevensey after their defeat at the Battle of Lewes (see Walk 9) and successfully withstood a siege by the son of Simon de Montfort. In 1399 the Constable of the Castle, Sir John Pelham, supported Henry Bolingbroke (later Henry IV) in his rebellion against King Richard II, and Sir John's wife, Lady Joan, defended Pevensey Castle against the King's forces. The castle later became a prison for the more distinguished of Henry IV's opponents.*

*Pevensey's last action was in 1588, when it was refortified and garrisoned to defend against the threat of the Spanish Armada. After this, the castle was left uninhabited and gradually fell into decay.*

Follow the path out through the Roman walls and down to a wooden gate.

*There is a fine view of the Roman walls here, seen almost in cross-section. They were 12 ft thick and had sandstone faces with an inner core of flint rubble for extra strength. Where you are passing through the walls was the main Roman gateway, on the landward end of the peninsula. The gate was 9 ft wide and arched with a gatehouse above. A ditch was cut across the neck of the peninsula to defend the landward side of the fort, part of which can still be seen to the right of the gate.*

Go through the kissing gate and keep straight on along the road, to reach the main road at the village green.

*This is the site of the Roman town of Anderida, which grew up within the fort but soon expanded outside the walls. After its inhabitants had been massacred in AD 491, the town was settled by the conquering Saxons, and now renamed Westham (from the Anglo-Saxon 'ham' or village, to the 'west' of the castle). By the time of the Norman Conquest Westham was a flourishing community, which is listed in the Domesday Book.*

Maintain the same direction past St Mary's church.

*St Mary's was founded in 1080. In Saxon times all but the most important buildings were made of wood and clay. The policy of the Normans was to overawe the conquered Anglo-Saxon population with their wealth and power, and constructing strong and imposing castles and churches made of stone were part of this policy. St Mary's church, along with the castle nearby, was a constant reminder of the power and permanence of the Norman invaders.*

Continue along the road, passing the Pevensey Castle public house, and 50 yards past the pub, turn right into Peelings Lane.

*In Roman and Norman times the flat land to your right was a sheltered harbour, sufficient to anchor the galleys used by the Romans to patrol the coast. Peelings Lane ran along a raised embankment, marshes to the left and harbour to the right, used by the Romans to carry a road connecting the town and fort to the mainland.*

Pass the village hall on your right and the village pond on your left. After the pond keep straight on along the road, to pass a 'derestriction' sign in 60 yards. Continue for another 200 yards and then turn right into the drive of Castle Farm.

❷   Go through the farmyard and over a stile beside a metal gate. Keep straight on across the brow of the hill ahead. Cross a stile in the far right-hand corner of the field and keep straight on to a footbridge on the far side of the next field. Go half-right to a stile 10 yards beyond the footbridge and climb steps up to the bypass. Cross the road with care and descend steps to a stile into a field.

*This area is known as Hankham Levels. Much of it is reclaimed marshland and today drainage ditches keep it relatively dry. The footpath follows the line of an embanked road, barely discernable now but in Roman and Norman times the only firm route across the marshland.*

Go slightly right of straight on, aiming at a gate in line with a dome just visible in the far distance (the Royal Observatory at Herstmonceux). Go through the gate and keep ahead to the next one. Cross the stile beside the gate and go half-right across the next meadow, aiming at a post seen in the field opposite.

❸   At the post DO NOT cross the footbridge but turn left along the embankment of Pevensey Haven.

*In 1066 the army of William the Conqueror followed the route you are now walking. The Norman army, some 7,000 men accompanied by 2,000 horses, disembarked at Pevensey and marched across the Hankham Levels to the raised banks of Pevensey Haven. Here they turned left, followed the river to Herstmonceux, and then swung east to occupy the port of Hastings.*

Follow the embankment, with Pevensey Haven on your right, for 1½ miles, passing through occasional gates. Eventually the path leaves the banks of the Haven. Keep ahead to pass close to an electricity pylon, then cross a stile to enter an enclosed footpath.

Follow the path past a farm and out to a lane.

❹    Turn right along the lane for 50 yards. Cross a bridge and turn right again with the lane.

*This is the end of the '1066 route'. The Normans continued ahead upstream, whilst you are returning to Pevensey.*

In 200 yards pass under electricity lines. Turn left with the lane (ignoring the gate to an Angling Club on the right), then 150 yards later, where the lane turns left again, turn right over a stile into a field. Turn left along the field boundary to a stile in the field corner. Cross the stile and go half-right across the field, diverging from the hedge on your left. You are aiming for a stile on the far side, 20 yards to the left of the right-hand corner of the field. Cross the stile and a footbridge and immediately turn right to walk along the field boundary, with trees and a ditch on your right. Pass through a gate and continue in the same direction along the next field to reach a gate on the far side. Go through and turn half-left to follow the left-hand hedge. DO NOT follow a grassy track into a field but keep the hedge close on your left hand, following a faint grassy path out to a green field gate leading into a lane.

❺    Turn right and follow the lane past a farm. Immediately after the farm buildings turn right through the gates of Chilly Farm and follow the concrete farm track. At the end of water on your left, turn left through a gate at a footpath post. Go half-right across the field to a stile on the far side. Cross the stile and footbridge into a field. Go half-right across the field, aiming at the walls of the castle seen ahead. Go through a gap in the hedge and continue in the same direction to reach the embankment of Pevensey Haven.

❻    Cross the footbridge and turn left along the embankment. After ⅓ mile, at a cross-ditch, leave the embankment and go through a gate 50 yards to the right. Continue ahead along an enclosed footpath, which turns right opposite a farm and leads to the bypass.

*In Roman and Norman times, the sea would have reached as far inland as here. You are now walking across what was the Roman harbour in AD 340. From here small warships patrolled the coast, guarding against*

*Saxon raiders. Six hundred years later, the port had disappeared. The sheltered anchorage, however, remained, and it was here that the Norman invasion fleet landed in 1066.*

**❼** Cross the bypass to a way-mark post opposite. Go through the gate and keep ahead along an enclosed footpath. Follow the footpath past houses and out to a road. Turn left and follow the castle wall back to the start.

**REFRESHMENTS**

The Royal Oak and Castle, next to the car park, has a large lunch menu and wide range of beers. It is very light and airy inside and has a large and attractive beer garden (telephone: 01323 762371). There are other pubs in Pevensey, as well as shops and a tearoom.

# Walk 6

# Bosham and the Last Days of Anglo-Saxon England

**Length: 5½ miles**

*Bosham harbour*

> **HOW TO GET THERE:** Bosham is 3 miles west of Chichester and just south of the A259.
>
> **PARKING:** The walk starts in the pay-and-display car park. Bosham Harbour.
>
> **MAP:** OS Landranger 197 (GR 805040).

## Introduction

This very pretty walk starts at Bosham, with its picturesque harbour, and fine Saxon church, and goes across open farmland and along wild creeks, affording views of Chichester Cathedral across the estuary. It returns past Fishbourne Roman Villa. The walk is flat, easy underfoot, and route finding is simple.

## HISTORICAL BACKGROUND

Bosham today is renowned as a beauty spot and marina, but in the 11th century it was the setting for some of the final acts of Anglo-Saxon England.

The 25 year reign of King Aethelred, known to history as 'the Unready', had seen England ravaged by Viking raids of ever greater intensity. When Aethelred died in 1016, England was war-weary and desperately in need of peace and stability. The nobles of England with little hesitation offered the crown to the Danish prince, Cnut.

Cnut, King of England and Denmark and soon Norway and Sweden as well, became the greatest figure in the northern world, the most important man in Europe after the Holy Roman Emperor. But in an age when kingship required face-to-face rulership, the price Cnut paid for this power was the need to elevate certain nobles as sub-rulers. England was divided between four such potentates, of whom Godwin, Earl of Wessex was the most significant. This division fatally wounded England's unity, and allowed Godwin in particular to rule almost as a king in his own fiefdom. Godwin provided a rich palace at Bosham for Cnut to use whenever he came into Wessex.

On Cnut's death in 1035, Earl Godwin became kingmaker, supporting both of Cnut's sons in turn onto the throne before, in 1042, smoothing the way for England's third king in seven years,

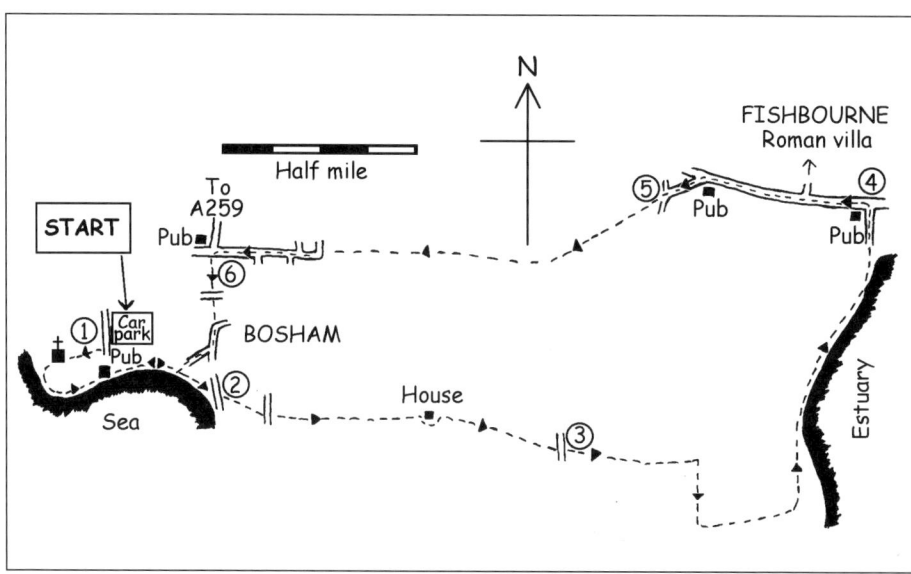

Edward 'the Confessor'. For the first decade of his reign Edward was under Godwin's thumb, even being forced to marry the Earl's daughter. Gradually, however, the King increased his power base and in 1051 was eventually able to force Godwin into exile. Godwin was allowed to return the following year and retired to Bosham, where he lived the last year of his life.

After Earl Godwin's death, his son Harold inherited his estates and title, and strengthened his hold on England. He became effectively warlord of the English armies, and saw himself as the obvious successor to his brother-in-law Edward. To combat this, it appears that Edward nominated William, Duke of Normandy as his heir and in 1065, taking advantage of a downturn in Harold's political fortunes, he forced Harold to accept this choice. Harold reluctantly sailed from Bosham Harbour to Normandy to swear an oath of allegiance to William.The scene was set for the Norman Conquest the following year.

## THE WALK

❶ From the car park entrance turn left towards the waterfront and immediately turn right into a footpath signed 'to Parish Church'. Note the manor house over the wall to your right.

*The manor house, Tudor with Jacobean additions, stands on the site of Cnut's palace. The Anglo-Saxon kings rarely had a fixed capital. Instead, they toured their realm, being supported by each of their lords in turn. The palace here was given to Cnut by Earl Godwin and used frequently by the King throughout his reign.*

Enter the churchyard and proceed to the church.

*The church of the Holy Trinity is the oldest site of Christianity in Sussex. The Emperor Vespasian used Bosham as the base camp for his invasion of the Isle of Wight in AD 79, and the town remained a Roman administrative centre. The first church was built when the Romans converted to Christianity, and the faith clung on in Bosham after the legions departed in AD 410. When St Augustine returned in AD 597 to reconvert England, he found a Christian monastery still surviving here.*

*The present church was started on the site of the monastery in the late 800s, and the nave dates from then. The tower was added in AD 980-1000 and the chancel was started in 1040, on the orders of Earl Godwin.*

*King Cnut's daughter, aged between 8 and 11, was drowned in the millstream behind the church in 1020 and is buried in Bosham church. A second Saxon coffin from the same era has been found in the church and is claimed to be that of Earl Godwin himself. Although Godwin lived here at the end of his life, he is known to have died in Winchester, and there is no evidence that his body was returned to Bosham for burial.*

*Holy Trinity is the finest Saxon church in Sussex, with a magnificent horseshoe-shaped chancel arch and unique chancel capitals. There is also a reproduction of relevant parts of the Bayeux Tapestry.*

Leave the church at the tower end and walk ahead to the shoreline.

*It is not known for certain if King Cnut ever really ordered the tide to turn back, and if he did, where this is meant to have occurred. It does seem likely that the event has some basis in truth, and Bosham Harbour, with its huge tidal mudflats, is the most likely venue, especially given the proximity to the palace Cnut regularly used. The question is, why did Cnut engage in such a bizarre act? There are numerous theories, but what is certain is that the*

*level-headed and astute King could not really have believed that the tide would turn at his command. It is possible that the affair was a carefully staged for the benefit of his courtiers to demonstrate the limits of his power.*

Turn left along the quay, with the water on your right, and follow the road along the shoreline, soon passing the Anchor Bleu Inn. Continue along the road to join an elevated footpath at a slipway. (NB: This road floods at high tide. If the road is underwater, follow the road along the side of the church, continuing past the Anchor Bleu and through an alleyway onto the elevated footpath, just above the water.)

*Holy Trinity church, Bosham*

*In 1065 Harold, son of Earl Godwin, sailed from Bosham to Normandy, having first prayed in Holy Trinity church for a safe return. Why he went to Normandy has been subsequently shrouded in mystery. The most likely explanation is that Harold, his political power at its lowest ebb, was ordered by Edward to go and swear fealty to William, Duke of Normandy, in a deliberate bid by the King to sabotage Harold's own aspirations for the crown. After the event, Harold was to claim that he was shipwrecked en route elsewhere and forcibly detained by William, and only released once he had sworn to acknowledge William as King Edward's heir. For whatever reason the oath had been made, on Edward's death in 1066 Harold promptly broke it, claiming it had been had given under duress, and took the crown. Nine months later, he was killed at the Battle of Hastings, and Duke William, now known as the Conqueror, became King of England. The shipwreck and oath are depicted in the Bayeux Tapestry, and in the copied panels to be seen in Holy Trinity church.*

Continue along the walled footpath across the head of the estuary to reach a road in front of a building labelled 'National School 1834'.

❷   Turn sharp left into 'The Drive' and after 10 yards, beside the first white bungalow on the right, turn right along an enclosed footpath and follow it to a lane. Cross the lane and keep straight along a footpath across a field. At the end of the field turn left and then right to join a track. Turn left along the track. At a house, DO NOT follow the track to the left of the house but instead follow the field edge across grass to pass the house on your left. Go around the house and continue along the field boundary, with the house and then a hedge on your left. In the field corner go through a gap in the hedge and maintain your same direction along an enclosed footpath to reach a road.

❸   Cross the road and keep straight on along a clear footpath aiming to the right of a line of trees seen ahead. (NB: This public footpath is marked on the 1:25 000 series OS maps, but unaccount-ably not on all editions of the 1:50 000 series.) Continue, with the line of trees on your left, until you reach a T-junction. Turn right and follow the grassy track between fields. At the end of the field on the right, at a fingerpost, turn left. Follow the track, soon a footpath, to the shore of the creek.

*There are fine views of Chichester Cathedral over the creek.*

Swing left, with the creek on your right. Soon follow a footpath along an embankment around the head of the creek. At the end of the embankment go right down steps and follow the path through a reed bed and past a millpond to reach the head of a lane. Turn left along the lane to reach the main road, with the Bull's Head pub on the corner.

**REFRESHMENTS**

The Anchor Bleu inn has a fine waterside location, with a riverfront terrace that provides excellent views over the estuary. It offers a range of good food (telephone: 01243 573956). Both the Blackboy Inn (telephone: 01243 575478) and the Bull's Head (telephone: 01243 839895) are passed en route in Fishbourne, and the Berkeley Arms (telephone: 01243 573167) towards the end of the walk. There are also shops and tearooms in Bosham.

❹    Turn left along the main road for ½ mile, passing a sign to Fishbourne Roman Villa on the right, to reach the Blackboy Inn, where you fork left into Old Park Lane. Where the road bends left and a side road joins from the right, keep straight on along a track.

❺    Follow the track between fields, ignoring all side turns, in a more-or-less straight line for ½ mile. The track eventually becomes a footpath and emerges at the corner of a lane. Keep ahead along the lane for ¼ mile, crossing Crede Lane on the right, and then Taylors Lane and School Lane on the left.

❻    Opposite a road on the right, with the Berkeley Arms on the corner, turn left into an enclosed footpath, with Miles House immediately on the left. When you reach a road, cross and continue ahead. On reaching Canute Road continue ahead along the road, and then turn right into Harbour Road. Turn right along the shore back to the start.

# WALK 7

# BATTLE ABBEY AND THE BATTLE OF HASTINGS 1066

**Length: 6½ miles**

*The gatehouse at Battle Abbey*

**HOW TO GET THERE:** Battle is 5 miles north-west of Hastings, on the A2100.

**PARKING:** The walk starts from the Mount Street pay-and-display car park in the centre of Battle, which is clearly signed from the main road.

**MAP:** OS Landranger 199 (GR 749159).

## INTRODUCTION

This fairly strenuous walk starts in the busy town of Battle, with the opportunity to visit the abbey, before going along the side of the battlefield. It then crosses undulating countryside, with a mixture of pleasant agricultural land and shady woods, using an ancient medieval trackway for part of the route.

## HISTORICAL BACKGROUND

Battle Abbey stands on the site of the most famous battle in British history, the battle of Hastings which saw the end of Anglo-Saxon England and the arrival of the Norman monarchs (described in more detail in Walk 6).

In Anglo-Saxon times, the rules of succession were not as clear-cut as they later became. 'Inheritance' – being related to the king – was not enough to ensure being the automatic heir. Two other factors

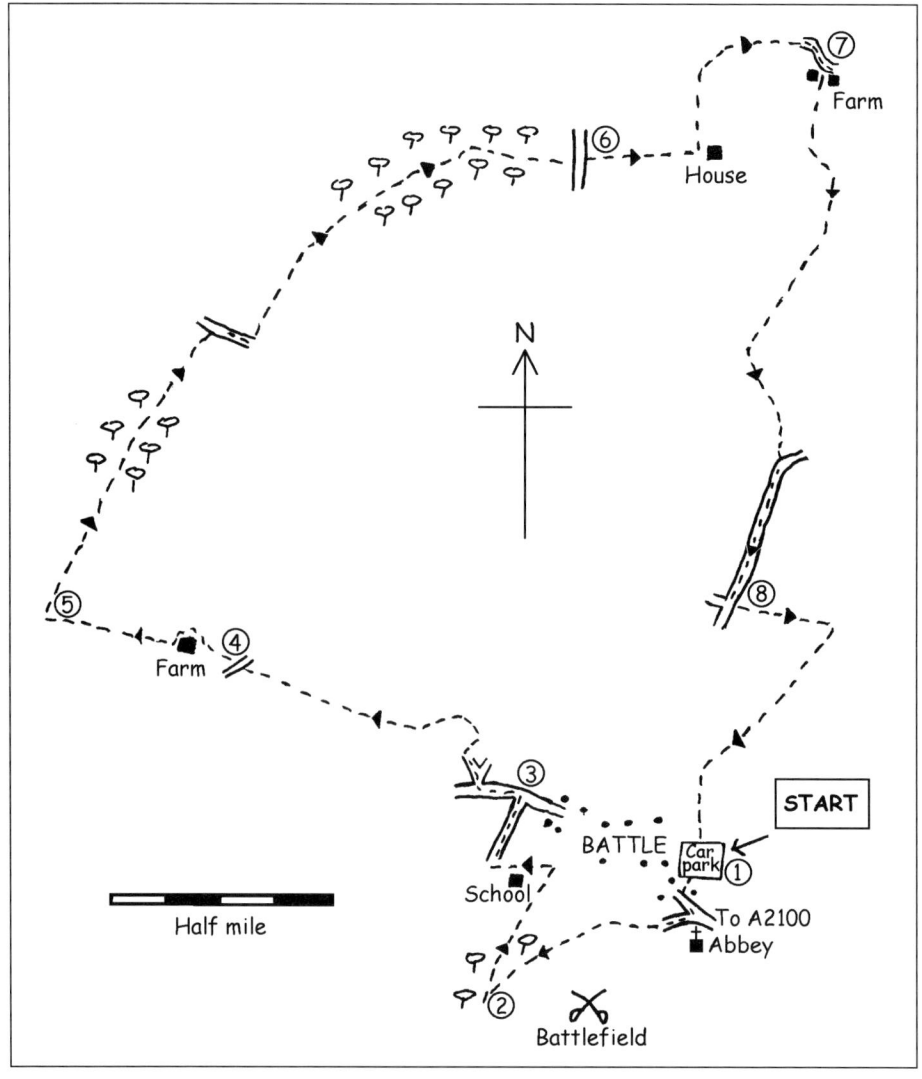

came into play when considering a claimant's right to the throne: 'election', where the claimant was offered the throne by the country or its ruling class; and 'designation', where the dead king had nominated his heir. Any claim was judged on the strength of one or more of these three elements.

When Edward the Confessor died in January 1066, there were several claimants to his throne.  Edward named as his heir William, Duke of Normandy, the grandson of his mother's brother, and thus William's claim was based on both designation and inheritance. Harold Hardrada, King of Norway, claimed the throne on the basis of an agreement with Edward's predecessor, which had designated him heir to the English throne. The weakest claim was that of Harold Godwinsson, Edward's brother-in-law and warchief of the English, who simply took the crown. His blood-tie was tenuous and he had been specifically excluded from the throne by Edward, but he was formally elected by his peers, anxious to avoid a foreign ruler. How many would have opposed the most powerful man in the kingdom in this circumstance is conjectural.

Harold knew that neither of his rivals would accept his seizure of the crown, and faced a threat from both north and south. Through-out the summer Harold waited in the vicinity of London for one or other rival to strike at him. In September Harold Hardrada, with 300 ships and 12,000 men, landed near York. King Harold, a military leader of note, rapidly assembled his army and marched north, covering 190 miles in just five days and taking the Norwegians totally by surprise. Harold inspired his weary troops to heroic efforts, and in a fierce battle at Stamford Bridge near York slew Hardrada and utterly routed his army.

Two days later, Duke William crossed the Channel with 7,000 men. He landed at Pevensey and then marched to outflank and seize the safe anchorage of Hastings. William then proceeded to lay waste the countryside around, to draw Harold to him. The English now faced the long march back from York to London, and then, after barely a pause, marched rapidly southwards, hoping to take William by surprise. On the night of 13th October, the English army was within six miles of Hastings. The Normans advanced to meet them, and the Battle of Hastings was imminent.

## THE WALK

NB: Be prepared for some muddy stretches in Wadhurst Lane (point 5).

❶  With your back to the public conveniences in the car park, turn left to reach the left-hand corner of the car park and follow the alley, signed 'town centre'. In the High Street turn left, crossing at the zebra crossing to reach the front of the abbey. It is open all year round from 10 am, closing at 6 pm from April to October and 4 pm from November to March. There is an admission charge; free to members of English Heritage.

*Battle Abbey stands on the actual battlefield, with the high altar on the exact position where King Harold fell. Building started in 1067, just months after the invasion, to fulfil a vow made by William the Conqueror, to build an abbey if his invasion of England was successful. The abbey is dedicated to St Martin and was consecrated in 1094 by Anselm, Archbishop of Canterbury (later Saint Anselm). William's battle sword and coronation robes were presented to the abbey by his son and successor.*

*Sixty monks were brought over from Marmoutier in Normandy to be the core of the abbey. It was given a privileged position amongst English religious houses, being exempt from any jurisdiction by the Bishop of its diocese, and having numerous and excessive feudal rights. Unusually, its abbots were mitred, a ceremonial headdress reserved for bishops, further fuelling resentment among the rest of the church establishment. The abbey had three parks, a vineyard and fishponds, and became the first commercial producer of cider in England.*

*The massive gateway was built in 1338 by the then Abbot as part of the fortifications of the town against French raids. The abbey was dissolved in 1538, part of the general Dissolution of the Monasteries.*

Facing the abbey, turn right and walk down the lane, the wall of the abbey grounds on your left. Continue past the abbey car park to a gate leading into a field. Follow the bridleway along the left-hand edge of the field.

*The actual battlefield was on your left. The hill along which you are walking is Senlac Hill, and it was here that King Harold drew up his forces on the morning of 14th October 1066. Harold had hoped to surprise William by the speed of his advance, but as his forces crested Senlac Hill they discovered the Norman army on Telham Hill opposite (in front of you across the now wooded valley), advancing to meet them. The two armies were evenly matched: the Normans had 7,000 men, professional soldiers and with a strong mounted contingent; the Saxon army of 10,000 men,* was the larger force, but comprised overwhelmingly foot soldiers, many of them conscripted for the one campaign.

Harold, instead of making a surprise attack, was forced to adopt a defensive position. Fortunately Senlac Hill was a naturally strong position. Although the slope in front is gentle, the ground in the valley below was marshy and the sides were steep, thus protecting Harold from the Norman cavalry. Additionally, the Saxons stood on higher ground, giving maximum advantage to their weapon of choice, the terrifying battle-axe.

The battle started around 10.30 am. Initially Norman archers were sent forward to fire arrows, which did little damage to the Saxons, sheltering behind a wall of overlapping shields. Next William ordered an all-out assault by infantry and cavalry. After ferocious hand-to-hand fighting the Norman left-wing lost heart and retreated. Many of Harold's troops broke from their defensive formation and poured down the hill in pursuit, only to be cut down by the Norman counter-attack.

The battle raged all day, with the Saxons beating off successive Norman attacks. Finally, as evening drew on, the Norman archers altered tactics, firing high into the air so that their arrows fell from above on the Saxons sheltering behind their shields. King Harold, along with many of his men, fell beneath this onslaught. Gradually Saxon losses mounted, until finally William ordered a charge by both infantry and cavalry. By sheer weight of numbers the Normans overwhelmed the weakened Saxon position.

Duke William had killed his rival and smashed the main Saxon army, but two more months of skirmishing lay ahead of him before he was finally crowned King of England on Christmas Day 1066. It was not until 1072 that the fighting finally finished and William the Conqueror was secure on his throne.

There is an excellent walk around the battlefield, with highly informative plaques at intervals to guide the visitor through the course of the battle. The walk is reached through the grounds of the abbey, entered via the gate already passed, for which there is an entrance charge.

❷   Go through a gate and immediately turn sharp right onto a footpath, crossing a stile into woods. Descend steps and turn right along a footpath. At a junction of paths in a few yards turn right through a pedestrian gate into a field. Continue straight on towards houses. At the end of the field bear left to emerge into a car park, with a school on your left. Cross in front of the school gates and continue forward along an enclosed footpath. At a mini roundabout in front of Saxonwood turn right along the road.

❸    At the A271 turn left. Cross the road and take the first turn on the right into Wellington Gardens. Bear left along the side of the gardens. At the end of the road keep ahead through a gap in the hedge to reach a crossing footpath. Turn right, initially along the side of an electricity installation. Emerge onto a wider track and turn right for 15 yards, then turn left along the drive to Kelklands. Follow the track as it passes to the left of the gates to Kelklands, and continue as it narrows to a path and takes you to a stile into a field. Keep ahead across the field, gradually diverging from the left-hand hedge and aiming at a farm seen on the far side of the valley. Eventually a footbridge comes into sight in the valley bottom. Cross the footbridge and continue to a stile, then keep ahead up the right side of a field. At the end go half-left over a drive to a gate labelled 'footpath'.

❹    Follow the enclosed footpath to a stile into a field. Keep ahead across the field, aiming for a gap in the hedge 20 yards to the right of buildings opposite. Go through the gap and keep ahead, to pass close along the side of a wall. Follow the wall and then a fence to a stile in the top left corner of the field, beneath an electricity pole. Cross the stile and follow a narrow path around the back of farm buildings to a stile leading onto a farm drive. Turn right along the drive and bear half-left through a gate into a green lane. Follow the lane to its end and keep ahead along the top edge of a field, with the hedge on your right. In the far right corner of the field, look for a stile, somewhat overgrown. Cross and descend to a T-junction.

❺    Turn right up a green lane, very overgrown at its start.

*This is Wadhurst Lane. This ancient trackway existed in 1066, and was one of the network of lanes that connected the villages and fields of the area. Harold's 10,000 strong army did not march as one mass but in small contingents, close enough together to reunite when necessary, but by being separate able to make maximum speed by utilising all possible roads. It is very likely that Wadhurst Lane was used by some of those Saxons hurrying towards Hastings.*

Follow the lane, often very muddy in its middle section. At the top of the slope, bear right with the lane through woods. Follow the lane to a road. Turn right along the road for 150 yards, then turn left through a gate next to the drive of 'Pegasus'. Follow the enclosed footpath. Cross a golf course drive and continue straight on, following a sunken path between trees.

*The sunken path is still the course of Wadhurst Lane.*

At a T-junction turn left for 5 yards and then right down the side of a fairway. A hedge, and the line of the lane, are close by on your right. In the bottom corner of the golf course, keep ahead into trees. Follow a broad bridleway through the woods for ½ mile, ignoring a clear uphill turn to the left, and follow the track out to a busy road.

*This road is the exact route followed from London to Hastings in 1066. King Harold had force-marched his army from York to London, where he began to immediately muster as many new troops as he could. He decided, wisely, that surprise was his best weapon and after only two days marched on towards Hastings. Many of the troops who had fought with him at Stamford Bridge had still not rejoined him when he left London.*

❻ Cross the road and go along the tarmac drive opposite. Follow the drive for 350 yards, then 10 yards before the brick gateposts of the house, turn left through an unmarked wooden gate (ignore a footpath to the right). Follow a drive for 30 yards then turn left behind a shed, opposite the back gate of the house. Follow the track through a metal gate into woods. Keep ahead and pass a tank and barn on your left. At a cross-track a few yards later, keep ahead. After 250 yards, keep ahead into a field and bear right, following the right-hand hedge. Views open up down the field on your left. Emerge onto an unmade track beside a cottage, and then follow the track as it curves between houses. At a junction in front of the white-painted Larkcroft, bear right.

**The route finding for the next small section is not obvious, and careful attention needs to be paid to the directions.**

❼ Some 50 yards after Larkcroft, turn right towards farm buildings. Almost immediately, turn left through a metal gate and keep ahead along the side of a barn, going under a corrugated iron roof. Keep the barn wall immediately on your right hand and follow it to reach a stile at the end of the barn. Cross the stile and maintain same direction into a field. Bear left down to a gate. Continue ahead down the side of the field, to a footbridge in the bottom left-hand corner. Cross the bridge and go half-right across the next field to a second footbridge. Walk uphill, passing a bush close on your left hand and a telegraph pole close on your right. At the

> **REFRESHMENTS**
>
> There are numerous pubs, cafés and shops in Battle. The Pilgrims Rest in the High Street provides good, hearty meals (telephone: 01424 772314), whilst nearby the King's Head, the oldest pub in Battle, is a quiet, oak-beamed pub offering good beers and limited food (telephone: 01424 772317).

brow of the hill bear half-right to a stile, then go diagonally left across the field to another stile in between trees. Maintain the same direction across the next field, aiming just to the right of a telegraph pole seen on the far side. Drop down half-left to a stile in the trees, in front of a corrugated shed. Turn left along the side of the shed and then continue, with a hedge and trees close on your left hand, to a stile leading onto a track. Turn left along the track for ¼ mile to reach a road.

❽   Turn right along the road, soon with a pavement, for 500 yards to reach Virgins Lane on your right. There is a telephone box on the corner. Turn left into an unmade road, signed 'Uckham Lane Nurseries'. Continue along the lane past the entrance to the nurseries. Shortly after, turn right across a stile at the gates to a caravan park, at a waymark post. Bear quarter-right and go along the side of a field, with a hedge on your left and the campsite behind it, to reach a stile. Cross the stile and keep ahead, closing on the left-hand hedge, to pass to the left of a grassy bank. Continue, with the hedge on your left, to reach a gap in the hedge in the left-hand corner. Go through the gap and maintain the same direction, with the hedge now on your right.

*Battle Abbey can be seen ahead to the left.*

At the end of the field, go through a kissing gate and continue in the same direction along an enclosed footpath. Cross over a cross-track and continue along the enclosed footpath to reach the car park.

# WALK 8

# AMBERLEY CASTLE AND THE POWER OF THE CHURCH

**Length: 5 miles**

*Amberley Castle*

**HOW TO GET THERE**: Amberley is 4 miles north-east of Arundel, just north of the B2139. The walk starts at the church in Amberley.

**PARKING:** There is plentiful roadside parking in the village, but please park with consideration for residents.

**MAP**: OS Landranger 197 (GR 027132).

## INTRODUCTION

This walk starts in picturesque Amberley, one of the most attractive villages in Sussex, before climbing onto the South Downs. The ascent is strenuous but the effort is rewarded by magnificent views. The return route is easy, a pleasant stretch beside the River Arun and then well-signposted field paths taking you to Amberley Castle.

## HISTORICAL BACKGROUND

The Norman kings expected their churchmen to be great feudal magnates, and Amberley Castle, home of the Bishops of Chichester, is a perfect illustration of this expectation.

After the Norman Conquest in 1066, King William's first aim was to ensure that his new subjects were properly subdued and that the realm could be protected, but without the crown bearing the cost of a standing army. To do this William introduced an idea new to English thought, the concept of feudalism, the theory that all land belonged to the king, and that land was held by others only by the king's gift, and in return for specified services. King William distributed the titles and lands of the Saxon aristocracy amongst his loyal barons and clergymen, but in return they were required to provide him with military and administrative services. They were to supply men and arms to fight when the King required, and also to govern their lands on the King's behalf, applying the Law and collecting taxes.

From the start the Norman Church assumed a military and political role as well as a spiritual one. Bishops were given vast tracts of land, but were expected to provide knights to fight for the King, to share the government of the land, and to attend the King's court and serve on his council. The Church soon came to hold 10% of the land

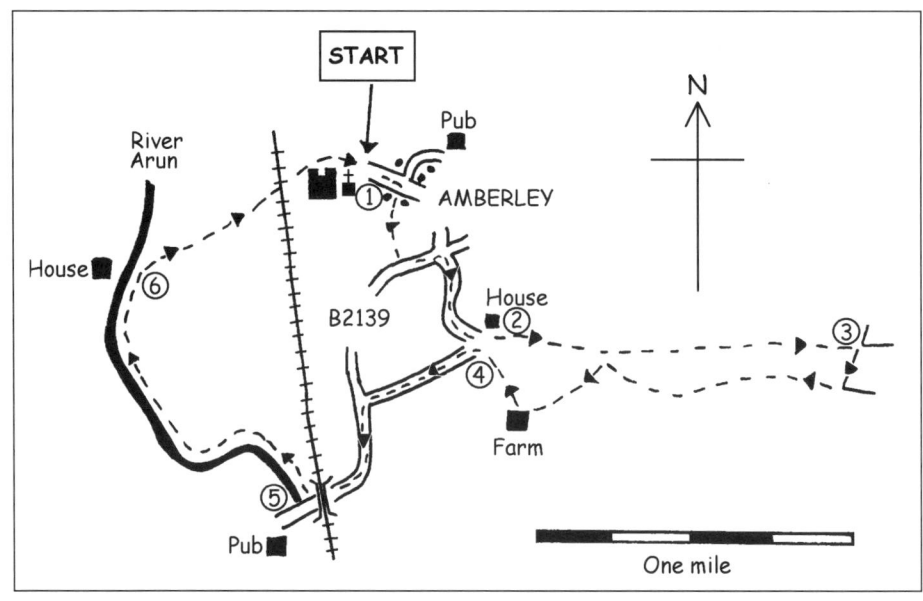

of England and receive 20% of the nation's income. Not surprisingly, many churchmen, especially in the higher reaches, spent far more of their time on their secular duties than on their spiritual ones.

One of the reforms that William instituted was that a bishop's 'seat' or headquarters should be in the largest centre of population in his diocese. The Saxon Bishop of Selsey therefore became the Bishop of Chichester. This required a new cathedral to be built in Chichester, and houses and palaces for the Bishop and higher clergy. In 1100 Bishop Luffa, who was in the process of building Chichester Cathedral, also built a manor house for himself at his feudal estate of Amberley. Over the next 250 years the manor house grew into the castle we see today.

## THE WALK

❶ With your back to the church gate, turn right along the main village street.

*The estates of Amberley had been given to the Saxon Bishop, later Saint, Wilfred in AD 680, and a church has been on this site since then. The present church of St Michael was built in the early 12th century, probably on the orders of Bishop Luffa, to serve as the church for his adjacent manor house.*

After 200 yards, opposite a side road on the left (to find the Black Horse, follow this side road around), turn right along an alley at a footpath sign. Follow the enclosed footpath to the main road. Turn left along the road for 120 yards, and then turn right up Mill Lane. At the top of the hill keep ahead past the gates of a house, ignoring both the South Downs Way sharp right and a footpath on the right.

❷ Continue for 50 yards past the house, then turn left up a steep track, signed 'South Downs Way'. DO NOT turn up to a metal field gate but keep right up a stony path to a wooden gate. Continue up the path onto Amberley Down.

*There are fine views from here down onto Amberley on the river plain below.*

At a T-junction with a track keep straight on. DO NOT turn right with the track in 30 yards but keep ahead, with a fence on your left, up the Down. Go through a gate and along an enclosed track for ¾ mile, with fine views over the Weald on your left.

❸   At a cross-track of the South Downs Way and a bridleway, turn right onto the bridleway (it is worth climbing the bank on your right for magnificent views all around). Just 5 yards after the fingerpost, turn half-right onto a descending path, with a bank on your right and trees on your left. At the bottom of the slope, at a fingerpost, go through a gate onto a track. Turn right along the track for ½ mile, with views now over a fine dry valley to the sea beyond. Where a track joins from the right, keep ahead through a gate. In 20 yards ignore a footpath ahead but bear left with the track and follow it towards a farm. Pass a barn on your left and go through a gate. Just before the farm, turn right down a track, then in 50 yards, at a T-junction, turn right down a surfaced lane.

❹   At a fork in the lane in ¼ mile, fork left. Follow the lane down to the main road. Cross to the pavement opposite and turn left down the road for ¼ mile, then pass under the railway. (The Bridge Inn, a brasserie and a teashop overlooking the river are just a few yards further down the road.)

❺   Immediately under the railway, turn right into a drive. At a footpath sign, cross a stile and follow the clear grassy track onto an embankment. Turn left to reach the river and follow the river bank to the right for a mile.

❻   At a fingerpost, with a house on the opposite bank of the river, turn right and aim for a gate in mid-field ahead. Cross a stile beside the gate and go half-left across the meadow, aiming for the tower of Amberley Castle, seen ahead. Go over a culvert and maintain the same direction to a gateway and fingerpost to the left of a tree, half-left ahead. Cross a stile by a gate and keep ahead along the track to go over the railway, then continue along a footpath beside a wall.

*You are now approaching Amberley Castle, whose huge curtain wall soon comes into sight. When the castle wall was built in 1377, a water gate was built into the wall you are approaching, to allow boats to enter. The Arun was less controlled in those days, and frequently the land was flooded right up to the castle walls.*

Follow the footpath to reach Amberley Castle. This is now a hotel. The gardens are open on occasions under the National Gardens Scheme, and the castle itself can be viewed by appointment, by ringing 01798 831992.

*The original manor house at Amberley, built here in 1100, was the country retreat of the Bishop of Chichester and also provided the administrative centre for his estates around Amberley. It was therefore a grand building from the time of its construction, and successive Bishops added to its facilities and luxury. In 1350 Bishop Rede greatly extended the house by adding a Great Hall and Solar. In 1377 he was granted a licence to 'crenellate', that is, to fortify the house, and convert it into a castle. This was at the height of the Hundred Years War, and was done in order to turn Amberley Castle into a stronghold guarding the strategic Arun gap against possible French raids; Rede was a bishop but also had a feudal duty to help in the military protection of the realm. The high wall in front of you was built at that time. The main entrance is on the other side of the castle, and is protected by twin drum-shaped towers with a moat in front.*

*After the Dissolution of the Monasteries in 1538 Amberley Castle was bought by the Lewknor family, owners of Bodiam Castle. During the Civil War it was held by the Royalists and fell to Parliament shortly after the capture of nearby Arundel. It was plundered and subsequently slipped into decay. The castle was purchased in 1893 by the Duke of Norfolk and restored.*

Continue past the castle on the enclosed footpath and go ahead along the drive to reach the church.

# WHO RULES ENGLAND?
# THE BATTLE OF LEWES 1264

**Length: 6 miles**

*The gatehouse leading to Lewes Castle*

**HOW TO GET THERE:** Lewes is on the A27, 9 miles north-east of Brighton. The walk starts at the Crown Inn, in the Market Square in Lewes. The square, which has the tourist information office in it, is in the middle of the High Street, dominated by the war memorial.

**PARKING:** There are several pay-and-display car parks in Lewes.

**MAP:** OS Landranger 198 (GR 416102).

**INTRODUCTION**

This delightfully varied circuit starts in Lewes, with its fine castle and remains of medieval walls, and then climbs gently onto the Downs, passing the site of the battlefield, relatively unchanged since 1264. An exhilarating walk across the Downs follows, with fine views all around, before descending to the village of Offham. The route concludes with a pleasant riverside stroll back into town.

**HISTORICAL BACKGROUND**

During his long reign, Henry III became increasingly unpopular with his barons. He was seen as unreliable and inconsistent, prone to unreasonable rages, extravagant and reliant upon favourites to enforce his rule. This antagonism towards Henry was part of a much wider issue, namely how much power should a king have to rule as he wished, and how much say in the government of the land should the hereditary nobility have. Henry's father King John had been forced to give some powers to the nobles in the Magna Carta, and Henry was deeply opposed to making any further concessions.

The issue came to a head in 1258, the 44th year of Henry's reign, when foreign adventures left him in desperate need of money. At a parliament held at Oxford, the barons refused to grant Henry any funds until he swore an oath accepting a council of nobles to act as

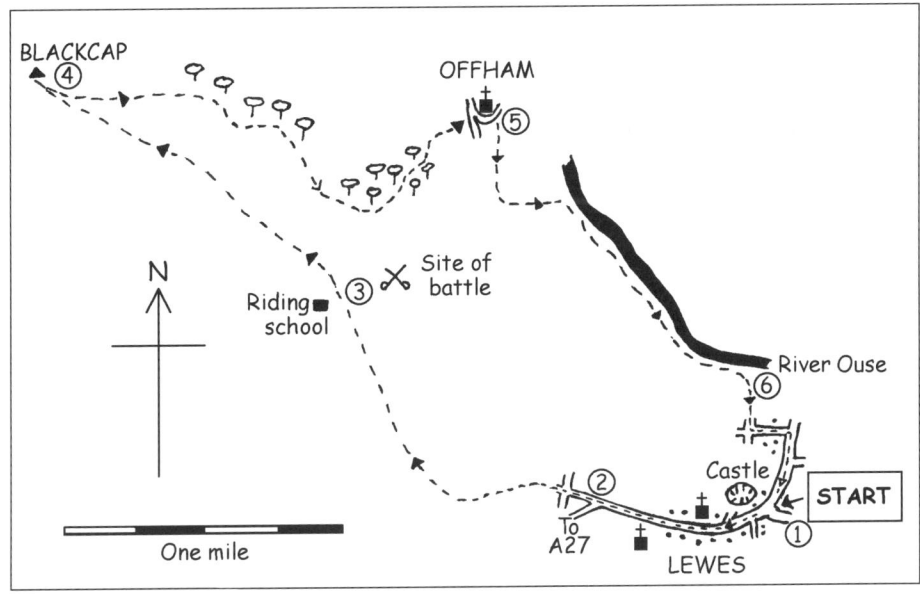

his official advisers, effectively giving the barons a formal share in the government. The King reluctantly gave his oath, but with no intention of keeping it.

Henry totally ignored the so-called 'Provisions of Oxford' and by 1264 had persuaded the Pope to annul his solemn oath. This high-handed action could not be accepted by a faction of the nobility, who found a leader in Henry's brother-in-law, Simon de Montfort, Earl of Leicester, the foremost soldier in England. These barons assembled an armed force with which to press their case.

London soon declared for the rebels, and de Montfort rapidly carried the conflict into Kent, leading an army to cut the King off from the Channel ports and foreign aid. The royal army was driven westwards into Sussex, pursued by de Montfort and subject to frequent small ambushes that drained men and morale. On 11th May 1264 the King's forces reached Lewes, with de Montfort's army close behind.

## THE WALK

❶   With your back to the war memorial and the Crown Inn on your right, walk along the High Street, soon passing the entrance to the castle on your right. Lewes Castle is well worth visiting. It is open to visitors from 10 am to 5.30 pm on Monday to Saturday and 11 am to 5.30 pm on Sunday. There is an admission charge.

*Shortly after the Battle of Hastings, William the Conqueror gave the town and manor of Lewes to his son-in-law, Earl William de Warenne. Earl William immediately set about building a strong castle to defend the strategically important valley where the River Ouse cuts through the Downs. The initial design of Lewes Castle was the traditional Norman layout, with an earthen mound, or 'motte', surmounted by a strong keep, and surrounded by a curtain wall that enclosed an open courtyard, or 'bailey'. Unusually, Lewes contains two mottes, with a strong keep on the western mound and a courtyard between the two. The original gatehouse, or barbican, was replaced in the 14th century by the enormous structure which can still be seen today.*

*In May 1264, Henry III and his forces marched into Lewes. The castle was already held for the King by John, Earl of Lewes, whose garrison had been reinforced by mounted soldiers led by Henry's son, Prince Edward. The King arrived on 11th May, and encamped his army to the south of the town, near the Priory of St Pancras. Although the 10,000 strong royal army was twice as large as the baronial forces pursuing them, they were tired and demoralised, and poorly led. King Henry and his leaders accepted the Earl's hospitality and stayed within the castle.*

*In the early morning of the 14th May, the baronial army led by de Montfort drew up in battle array on Offham Hill, overlooking Lewes to the north. Prince Edward immediately mustered his troops and marched out of the castle and down through the town's north gate, straight towards the enemy. His father the King was left to gather the bulk of the royal army and follow on behind.*

Continue along the High Street, soon passing St Michael's church on your right, and then passing Pipe Passage.

*The High Street still follows the same line as it did in 1264, and the 13th century church of St Michael has altered little since Henry III and his bodyguard rode out from Lewes Castle to meet up with their army. Glance up Pipe Passage as you pass: medieval Lewes was full of such narrow alleyways, known as 'twittens' leading off the High Street. In Henry's time the town was surrounded by a strong wall, and Pipe Passage ran along its inner side. The Westgate, through which Henry exited, was just beyond Pipe Passage, and stood until the 1700s.*

Continue along the High Street, passing the Pelham Arms and St Anne's church.

*St Anne's is the oldest church in Lewes. Its tower was built in 1150, the body of the church a few years later. It was outside St Anne's that King Henry and his bodyguard waited for the bulk of his army, which had been camped at St Pancras' Priory, just beyond the southern walls of Lewes. Once united with his forces, the King followed the route you are now taking, open fields in 1264, towards Offham Hill.*

❷　Where the road forks, by the Meridian public house on the right, fork right, signed 'Haywards Heath, East Grinstead'. After 100 yards, at a T-junction, cross the main road and go up Spital Road opposite. At the top of the lane, keep ahead up a bridleway, passing Heath Stables on your left. About 100 yards past the stables, at a fork in the path, bear right at a bridleway post. Follow the clearly marked bridleway to the top of the slope and along the crest of the Downs, to approach riding stables on the summit of Offham Hill.

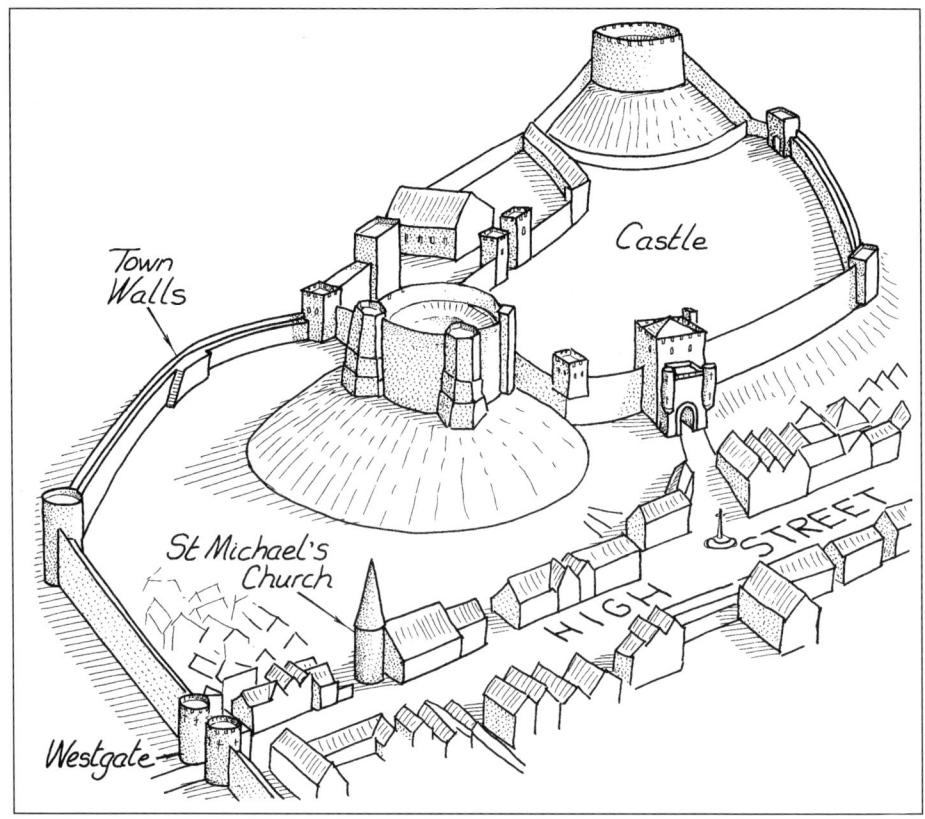

*Medieval Lewes*

*On 14th May 1264 the army of Simon de Montfort was drawn up on the summit of Offham hill, facing towards you, 5,000 men and 600 horses. His right flank was where the riding stables now stand, the rest of his army spread out to your right across the crest of the slope. Prince Edward and his force, mainly 1,500 mounted knights, charged up the slope to your right from the direction of the castle, which you can see in the distance. They shattered the left flank of de Montfort's army, raw recruits for the most part, and pursued them from the field. The rest of the royal army, some 8,000 men led by the King, came up the slope you have climbed to meet the seasoned veterans who comprised the remainder of de Montfort's force. After several hours of fierce fighting the royal army lost its nerve and broke. It fled back down towards Lewes, hotly pursued.*

❸    Keep ahead between the stables and paddocks, and continue along the broad track, gradually climbing. After ¾ mile, pass a National Trust 'Blackcap' sign and then pass through a gate onto the open downland of Mount Harry. After 600 yards, at a waymark post, keep straight on, aiming for gorse bushes and a stand of trees seen on the skyline ahead, the summit of Blackcap. Proceed to the triangulation point that marks the summit, for magnificent views all around.

*Simon de Montfort had broken his leg the previous December, and had been carried on his campaign in a closed carriage. Although by May 1264 he had recovered, and could lead his troops in person from horseback, he hoped to conceal this fact from his opponents. His carriage was conspicuously parked beneath his banner here on the summit of Blackcap, lulling his opponents into the belief that de Montfort was not present on the battlefield.*

❹  From the triangulation point, go back virtually the way you came for a few yards, keeping gorse bushes close on your left, and then veer left to pick up a clear track, running close to the steep wooded slope on your left. Follow this track for ¾ mile, to pass through a gate. Continue ahead, soon descending between gorse bushes. Keep right at a waymark post and descend, emerging from the gorse. Keep straight on to a clear track on the opposite side of a grassy clearing. Follow the track through the trees. Immediately afterwards, DO NOT turn right through the fence but keep ahead, the fence close on your right. At the end of the fenced enclosure go through a gate. Ignore a clear path going half right uphill, but instead go half-left, to the corner of woods seen ahead.

*The crest of the skyline ahead was where de Montfort's left flank stood on 14th May 1264, facing away from you. They were mainly raw troops, recruited in London, who had not seen combat before. They broke in face of the charge by Prince Edward's 1,500 mounted knights and fled down the slope to your left, towards the hamlet of Offham (where the church can now be seen). Prince Edward and his cavalry followed in hot pursuit.*

At the corner of the woods, turn sharp left at a waymark post and follow a path along the edge of the woods, with the trees close on your left. In 150 yards, follow the path as it turns left into the woods. Follow the clear path through the trees, descending slightly and ignoring side turns. Leave the woods via a gate and turn left down a track, continuing out to the road at Offham. Cross the road and turn left for 50 yards, and then turn right down a side road leading to the church.

*The terrified survivors of de Montfort's left wing fled down the slope you have just descended and sought shelter in the hamlet of Offham and the surrounding fields. Prince Edward's cavalry, in total disarray by the time they had pursued the fleeing soldiers down the hill, were finally called back into order, turned around and marched back up the hill. By the time they reached the summit, the King's forces had been chased from the field, and the battle had been lost.*

❺   Pass the church and where the road bends left, keep straight on at a fingerpost onto a track. Follow the track down through trees. At the bottom of the slope, turn left across a culvert to cross a stile beside a gate. Keep ahead, with a stream on your right. Go under the railway to reach the river. Turn right along the river bank for ¾ mile, until reaching a footbridge over the river.

❻   Do not cross the bridge, but turn right along a tarmac path, passing a waterway on your right, to reach the main road.

*The waterway is called the Pells, and is the remains of channels that provided water for a medieval corn mill. This waterway was here in King Henry's day, although the land between it and the river would have been poorly drained marshland. The main road follows the line of the old town walls.*

Turn left along the main road, to reach a T-junction just past a car park. Turn right into North Street and follow this road back to the war memorial.

*The death toll at the Battle of Lewes amounted to 2,800 men, many of them royal troops who drowned trying to escape across the marshy River Ouse after the battle. King Henry and Prince Edward were put under 'house arrest' and De Montfort became de facto ruler of England, governing in the King's name and attempting to put the country's administration and finances back on an even keel. His rule was popular with the middle classes, but was opposed by many amongst the nobility, either through jealousy of de Montfort's power or loyalty to the King. Foreign monarchs and the Pope also stirred up trouble for de Montfort.*

*The following year, Prince Edward escaped, and raised another army amongst discontented nobles in the Welsh Marches. John, Earl of Lewes had fled to France after the Battle of Lewes, but returned to join the Prince. Edward was no longer the impetuous youth seen at Lewes, but had grown into a fine general. In August 1265 De Montfort marched with his forces from his main castle in Kenilworth, but was outmanoeuvred and trapped at Evesham. In a short but bloody battle de Montfort died, together with his son and 4,000 of his men. Henry III was restored to his throne and reigned, unchallenged, for another seven years.*

> **REFRESHMENTS**
>
> Within Lewes there are many pubs serving food, including the Crown Inn (telephone: 01273 480670), and also several tearooms and numerous shops. The Pelham Arms, passed en route, has a wide range of cooked meals and also ploughman's lunches served within comfortable surroundings (telephone: 01273 476149).

# WINCHELSEA, THE RISE AND FALL OF A PORT

### Length: 5½ miles

*Town Gate, Winchelsea*

| HOW TO GET THERE: | PARKING: There is ample | MAP: OS Landranger 189 |
|---|---|---|
| Winchelsea is on the A259 Hastings-Rye road. The walk starts from the church in the centre of Winchelsea. | roadside parking in Winchelsea, but please park with consideration for residents. | (GR 904174). |

## INTRODUCTION

This walk starts in the historic town of Winchelsea, and then descends to cross open salt meadows to Rye, passing Camber Castle en route. It returns through fields to Winchelsea, following the old line of the coast in 1288. Walking is easy, with one steep but short ascent at the end.

## HISTORICAL BACKGROUND

The confederation known as the 'Cinque Ports' came into being in early Norman times, when five (or 'cinq' in French) ports – Hastings, Romney, Hythe, Dover and Sandwich – banded together, for mutual protection at sea and to enhance their trade. Ships were privately owned, but shipowners operated within rules set down by the confederation. At a time when there was no national navy, successive monarchs used the fleets of the Cinque Ports whenever ships were needed, hiring them not with cash but by granting privileges, such as the exclusive rights to carry certain imports and exports. By the end of the reign of King John (1216) the Cinque Ports fleet was England's unofficial navy, controlling the Channel and with it the lucrative trade with the Continent. To gain access to that trade, other ports along the coast of Sussex and Kent applied to join the confederation.

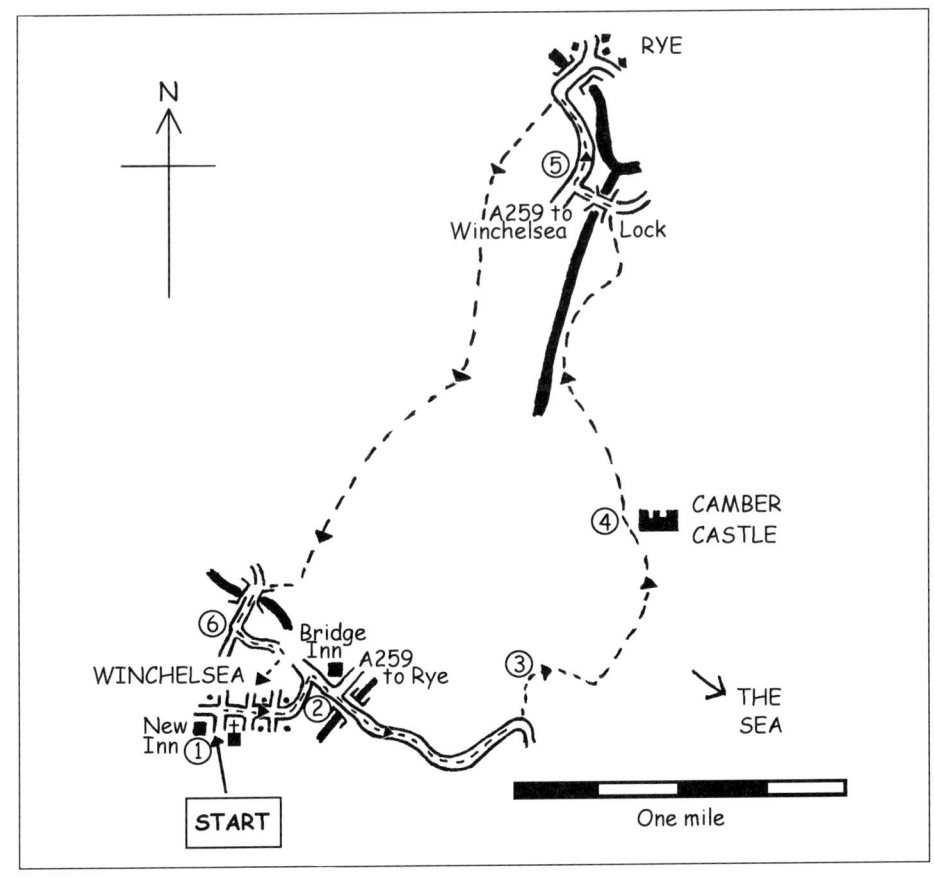

Winchelsea soon rose to become one of the most important of the Cinque Ports. When Edward I raised a fleet to fight the French, Winchelsea provided 13 of the 50 Cinque Ports ships, by far the largest single contingent. The importance of the port to the nation was recognised after 1287, when a ferocious storm devastated the town, hastening a process of gradual coastal erosion that had been going on throughout the century and washing away many houses. King Edward immediately gave vigorous aid, in the form of surveyors, engineers and most importantly money, and an entirely new town was built. The old site, on an eroding shingle beach, was abandoned, and instead a new site on a raised peninsula was chosen. Wide streets were laid out on a grid-iron pattern, and within each square thus formed a large plot of land was assigned to each household. The town was surrounded by impressive fortifications, incorporating the latest thinking upon military architecture.

Unfortunately, these precautions were not enough to protect the town. Winchelsea was attacked seven times by the French in the 14th and 15th centuries, and each time the attackers were able to enter, pillage and burn the town. Each time it recovered, and continued to play a vital role in the defence of the south coast against invasion. Winchelsea was finally destroyed, not by the French but by the sea. Inexorably, the coastline receded, sand and shingle gathered across the harbour mouth, and salt marshes developed along the beaches. By the end of the 15th century the port had ceased to be usable, and Winchelsea's great days were over.

## THE WALK

❶   With your back to the New Inn, walk straight ahead down the road, with the church on your right and the museum on your left. The museum is open from May to September daily, 10.30 am to 12.30 pm and 2.30 pm to 5.30 pm, afternoon only on Sundays. There is an admission charge.

*The church of St Thomas à Becket was planned on a magnificent scale when the town was laid out in 1288, and royal funds provided for its construction. It was never finished, and furthermore suffered damage during the French raids. The chancel, side chapels and the ruins of the aisles still remain. Much later, this church was the site of John Wesley's last open air sermon in 1790.*

*The church of St Thomas à Becket*

*The museum is located in the Old Court Hall, also built with royal funds in 1288, and later added to in the 15th century. This was the courthouse and also the gaol of Winchelsea. Today it houses an interesting history of the Cinque Ports.*

Soon reach the Strand Gate.

*The Strand Gate was one of three original town gates and gave access to the port. The massive gatehouse was originally set into equally massive town walls, long since pulled down. This gate has the dubious fame of being the only one through which the French **did not** enter Winchelsea in any of their seven raids. Next to the gate is the Lookout, built to provide a vantage point for a watchman in the days of the French Wars. From here there are excellent views of the whole coast, and on a clear day the French coast is visible.*

Go through the gate and down the hill. At the bottom of the hill turn right along the busy main road, past the Bridge Inn.

*Behind the inn is the meandering River Brede. In 1288 this was its estuary and the port of Winchelsea was built here, just below the ramparts of the town walls.*

❷   Immediately past the inn, where the road bends left, turn right along a side road, signed ' Winchelsea Beach'. In a few yards, cross the Royal Military Canal. Continue along the road for ½ mile.

*The Royal Military Canal was built in 1803, part of England's defences against the threat of invasion by Napoleon. In 1288 this was the coastline. The sea lapped the cliffs behind you, on which Winchelsea is built, and the River Brede entered the sea at this point. The flat expanse of land to your right was open ocean in 1288.*

Where the road bends sharp right, keep straight on along a track. It is marked ' Private Road, no access to beach', but it is a public footpath. Bend left with the track, ignoring a stile on the right on the bend, and continue along the track.

*The coast of Sussex has faced invasion threats throughout its history. Winchelsea was fortified against the French in 1288; soon we pass Camber Castle, built as a defence against the French by Henry VIII. To your left is the Royal Military Canal, the 19th century defensive moat, and behind that can be seen a World War II pillbox, survivor of the last invasion threat.*

❸   At the gate to River Brede Farm campsite, bear right with the tarmac track. Follow the track, soon gravelled, until you bear left past a farm entrance and through a gate. Just through the gate, take the left fork of two tracks.

*Camber Castle can be seen ahead, with Rye visible on the hill behind. The ridge on the left was the coastline in 1288: Rye and Winchelsea, on their respective hills, faced one another across open ocean. The original town of Winchelsea stood here, upon a shingle spit of land stretching out into the sea.*

Follow the track to Camber Castle, finally passing through a metal gate to approach the castle itself. The interior of Camber Castle is open on Saturday and Sunday afternoons July to September, 2 pm to

5 pm. Visits can be arranged by ringing the ranger on 01797 223862. The outside, in many ways the castle's most spectacular aspect, can be walked around at any time.

*By the 16th century the sea had retreated, leaving Winchelsea high and dry behind salt marshes and shingle flats. Camber Castle was built in 1539 on the water's edge. It was constructed by Henry VIII in the new flower-shaped design characteristic of castles of the time, which gave maximum protection against cannon balls. It had a garrison of 42 men and was one of a number of forts that lined the south coast. As the sea continued to retreat, Camber was left ever further inland, until today it is a mile from the sea. It was finally abandoned in 1627.*

❹   After viewing the castle, return towards the metal gate. Just before the gate, turn sharp right and follow the track, the fence close on your left. Go through two metal gates and over a drainage channel. Continue ahead along a raised path, the drainage channel on your right. Follow the path as it passes between the channel on the right and the canal on the left. Go through a gate and bear left at a fork, following the canal bank. Keep ahead through a metal pedestrian gate to reach a track. Bear left along the track, still heading towards Rye seen ahead. On reaching a road, turn left over a lock. Keep ahead to a T-junction, where you turn right.

❺   Follow the road to reach a garage. Cross the road and continue towards Rye for 20 yards. (To visit Rye, cross the bridge to the harbour and Old Town.) For the walk itself, turn left down a track between houses and a bungalow, just before a green road sign. DO NOT follow the road around the bend towards the bridge, and IGNORE a footpath sign at the end of the bridge. Follow the track, initially tarmac, past a farmhouse. Turn left with the track, now unsurfaced, at a fingerpost.

*The cliffs to the right mark the shoreline in 1288. Winchelsea can be seen on the headland ahead.*

Go through a metal gate and keep ahead across a field to a gate on the far side. Cross a stile by the gate and keep ahead, a drainage ditch as close on your right hand as the crops will allow. At the end of the cropfield, cross a footbridge into a large meadow. Continue ahead, initially following the drainage ditch on your right hand. Where the ditch peters out, maintain the same direction, aiming for a metal-railed footbridge on the far side. Cross this footbridge and maintain the same direction, with another drainage ditch now on your right. Where the ditch veers right, continue straight on

along a clear path across the field, aiming all the while for Winchelsea on the hill ahead. Cross a footbridge at a waymark and maintain the same direction across the next large field. Near the far side of the field, bear right towards a white fence in front of bungalows. Cross a stile and turn left along the quiet lane, crossing a bridge.

*The bridge is over the River Brede again, the coastline in 1288. When the new town of Winchelsea was laid out, the harbour was built along the banks of the river below the cliff ahead. Each merchant was allotted his own warehousing space in the port.*

❻    At the road junction turn left along the main road for 300 yards. Just opposite the first house on the left, cross the road and climb steps up the bank. At the top of the bank follow a footpath out into Winchelsea. Keep ahead along the street and take the first turning on the right to return to the church.

*The grid-iron pattern of streets laid down in 1288 can clearly be seen on this short walk back through Winchelsea. The immediate impression is of the width of the streets, most unusual in a medieval town. The houses of the important merchants were concentrated in this northern sector, and many are still to be seen. The road level was much lower in 1288 than today, and stone steps led up to the front doors.*

*It is worth walking around Winchelsea. An information board in front of the church gives a plan of the town and the major points of interest, and an informative guidebook is on sale in the museum.*

# WALK 11
# BODIAM CASTLE AND THE HUNDRED YEARS WAR

**Length: 3 miles**

*Bodiam Castle, the pinnacle of medieval architecture*

**HOW TO GET THERE:** The walk starts in Ewhurst Green, which is on a minor road, 2 miles south of Bodiam and 3 miles west of Northiam.

**PARKING:** There is plentiful roadside parking in the village, but please park with consideration for the residents.

**MAP:** OS Landranger 199 (GR 796247).

## INTRODUCTION

This short walk starts in the quiet village of Ewhurst Green, and gently descends through fields to the River Rother, with fine views of Bodiam Castle. It then follows the river bank to reach the castle itself, before returning across rolling fields to the start. Walking is gentle, with one easy descent and one easy ascent.

## HISTORICAL BACKGROUND

The castle of Bodiam, completed in 1388, represents the final and most perfect phase of medieval castle design in England, but it never saw action as a fortress.

The castle's founder was a Sussex knight, Sir Edward Dalyngrigge. Born the son of minor landowning gentry near East Grinstead, he went as a soldier to seek fame and fortune in France during the early campaigns of the Hundred Years War. His bravery was rewarded with a knighthood by King Edward III and he returned to England both famous and rich with plunder taken from the French. In 1377, now a

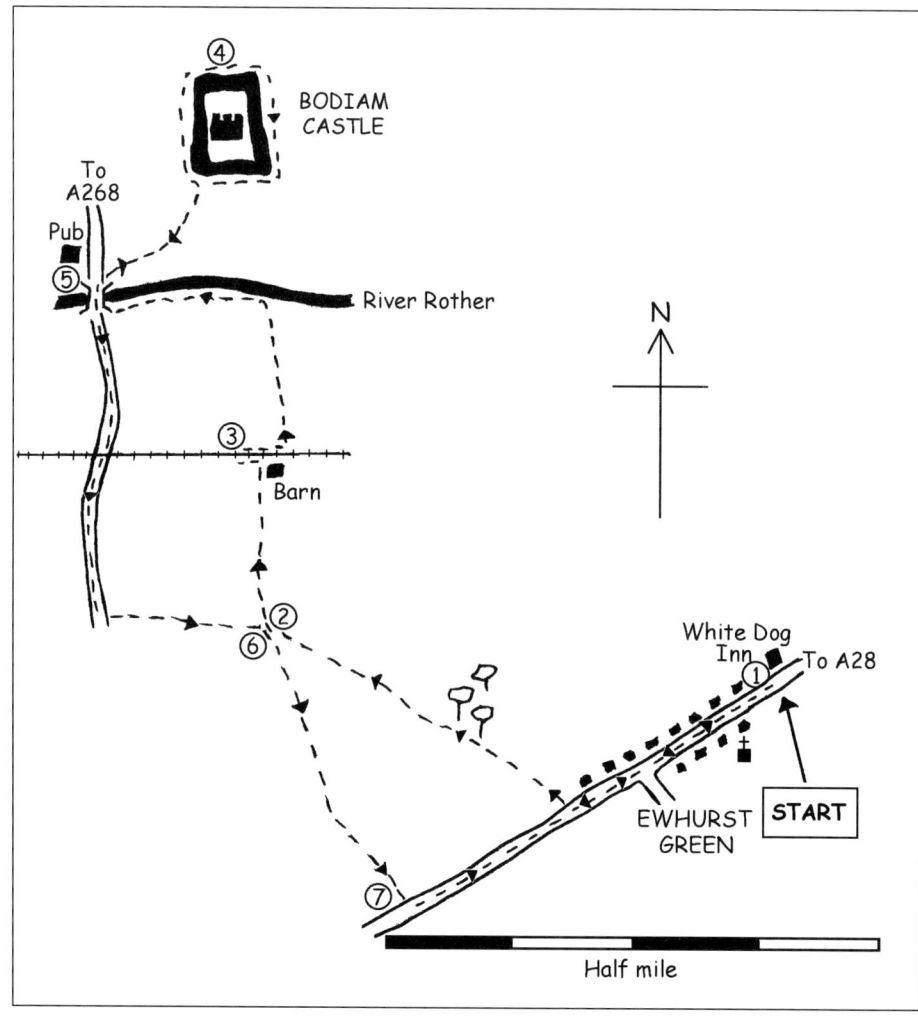

man of some importance in the county, he married Elizabeth Wardeux, heiress to the manor of Bodiam. This added still further to Sir Edward's wealth and standing, and he became an important figure in the government of Sussex.

The Hundred Years War was not a period of continual fighting but rather sporadic campaigns by the English across the plains of northern France and intermittent French raids upon the southern coast of England. In 1372 the English had lost control of the Channel, Rye was sacked by the French in 1377, and Winchelsea in 1380. The River Rother, which in those days was navigable as far inland as Bodiam, provided an inviting route into the heart of Sussex for French warships, and so in 1385 Sir Edward was given permission by King Richard II to fortify his manor house.

Instead, Sir Edward decided to start from scratch and build a castle which would not only meet the King's requirement for a stronghold to defend a vulnerable spot on the coast, but would also provide a residence suitable for a man of his wealth and standing. The result was the magnificent edifice seen today.

The castle was never put to the test. By the time of its completion, the English had regained control of the Channel and French raids ceased. The castle did however serve as a home and headquarters for Sir Edward until his death in 1395, and later for his son John.

## THE WALK

❶   With your back to the White Dog Inn, turn right and walk along the village street, passing the church and a side lane on your left. Soon pass 'The Old Library' on your right, and 20 yards later, turn right through a kissing gate. Walk down the left-hand side of the field. At the bottom of the slope, just before trees, turn left through a kissing gate, partly hidden behind a holly bush. Cross the stile ahead and turn half-left along the field edge, with the fence on your right, to reach a stile beside a metal field gate, to the right of a tumbled-down shed. Keep straight on down the next field, with the fence still on your right, to reach a stile in the field bottom, at a signpost.

❷   Cross the stile and turn right for 40 yards to go over a footbridge in the field corner. Ignore a gate and concrete bridge on your left, but keep ahead, with the hedge on your left. Soon a barn comes into sight ahead. Cross a footbridge in front of the barn and keep ahead along the side of the barn to a metal field gate in front of the railway.

Turn left for 5 yards and cross a stile beside a metal gate. Immediately turn right to carefully cross the railway line via two stiles.

❸   Turn right, with the railway immediately on your right, to reach the corner of the field. Here turn left and walk towards the castle, with a hedge now on your right, aiming towards a prominent metal gate. At the gate turn left along an embankment on the river bank. At the end of the embankment, cross a stile onto a road and turn right across the bridge. At the end of the bridge turn right, signed 'footpath to castle'. Cross the car park and go through a gate onto a broad path leading to the castle (the ticket office is on the far side). Between February and October Bodiam Castle is open daily from 10 am to 6 pm (or dusk); between November and January it opens on Saturday and Sunday, 10 am to 4 pm. There is an admission charge; free to National Trust members.

*Bodiam Castle represented the culmination of medieval military architecture, before the advent of gunpowder made all the defences that had gone before redundant. Unlike traditional Norman castles, Bodiam does not consist of a separate keep and encircling walls. Instead, the walls* **are** *the castle. They are massive in order to withstand bombardment, with a strong circular tower at each corner, defended by a wide moat to disrupt assault and to prevent the undermining of the walls, and with overhanging parapets with holes set into their floors, through which missiles could be dropped on any attackers who reached the walls. The central tower you first see as you approach the castle is only the postern gate: the main entrance with its massive gatehouse is on the opposite side of the castle. There was a small harbour in front of the postern gate, providing safe anchorage beneath the castle walls for sea-going ships. On the outer wall of the postern is carved a shield, that of Sir Robert Knollys, under whom Sir Edward served when fighting in the French War.*

*However, Bodiam was never used against the French, its intended foe. For a century it was home to the Dalyngrigges and their successors, the Lewknors. In 1483 it was briefly held by Sir Thomas Lewknor against King Richard III, but he surrendered without a fight. It was reduced to a ruin in 1643 by Parliamentarian forces during the Civil War, to prevent its use by the Royalists.*

Bear left and walk around the castle to reach the gatehouse.

*The main gatehouse has three drawbridges, defended by two fortified bridgeheads or barbicans as well as the gatehouse itself. On the outside face of the gatehouse are carved three shields. The central shield is that of Sir Edward Dalyngrigge, and to its left is the shield of the Wardeux family. The third shield bears the arms of the Radynden family, relatives of Sir Edward.*

> **REFRESHMENTS**
>
> The White Dog Inn in Ewhurst Green offers food all day and a range of beers (telephone: 01580 830264). The wood-panelled front bar, with its flagstone floors, is walker-friendly, whilst a large beer garden offers a good view of Bodiam Castle. Halfway around the walk there are tearooms at the castle, also a pub nearby, the Castle (telephone: 01580 830330).

❹ Follow the footpath around the moat and return to the car park. Continue out to the road opposite the Castle public house.

❺ Turn left along the road and recross the bridge. Continue along the lane for 350 yards to cross the railway at a level crossing. Continue up the lane for a further 200 yards. Opposite the drive to Quarry Farm, turn left into a drive, with a high stone wall on your right and hedge on your left. Emerge from the enclosed drive, with a wooden fence on your left and an oast house in front. Immediately turn right over a stile. Cross the field to a stile opposite, just in front of a telegraph pole. Go half-left across the corner of the next field to another stile. Cross the stile and continue ahead down the field, with the fence on your left and the houses of Ewhurst Green seen on the skyline ahead. In the bottom corner of the field go through a gate and turn right for 5 yards to a stile and footbridge. Cross the footbridge and bear left towards the stile and signpost, passed on your outward journey.

❻ Cross the stile and immediately turn right. Walk uphill, with the fence close on your right. In the top right-hand corner of the field, cross a stile beside a gate and walk up an enclosed track, passing a house on your left.

❼ On reaching a lane, turn left and follow it back into Ewhurst Green.

# COWDRAY HOUSE, THE RISE OF THE TUDOR NEW MEN

**Length: 3½ miles**

*Cowdray House*

---

**HOW TO GET THERE:** Midhurst is on the A286, north of Chichester.

**PARKING:** The walk starts from the North Street car park (free) on the A286 on the northern outskirts of Midhurst.

**MAP:** OS Landranger 197 (GR 888217).

---

## INTRODUCTION

This easy walk starts in Midhurst and passes the spectacular ruins of Cowdray House, before crossing through pleasant countryside, with lovely views of the rolling Greensand landscape. It returns across a golf course, once the deer park of Cowdray House, affording fine views over the house and countryside.

## HISTORICAL BACKGROUND

Cowdray House owes its manificent to the FitzWilliam family, who came to prominence under the Tudors.

The accession of Henry Tudor to the throne in 1485 as Henry VII effectively ended the Wars of the Roses. The main impacts of the Wars had been in the collapse of central government, and a disproportionate degree of slaughter amongst the ruling classes. One of the new King's first tasks was to restock the aristocracy from amongst the ranks of his supporters. These 'new men' that Henry elevated to the peerage were a different breed to the old nobility. Many came from the ranks of the lesser gentry, often with backgrounds in commerce rather than feudal militarism. The new Tudor aristocracy contained men of administrative ability, able to undertake the task of recreating England as a trading and industrial nation.

The heart of Tudor government was the Royal Council. Initially this was a fluctuating body of personal advisers to the King, which gradually grew in importance. Under Henry's successor Henry VIII the council had evolved into an inner ring of some twenty advisers who followed the King wherever he went, and an outer ring that remained in London and undertook the daily administration of the

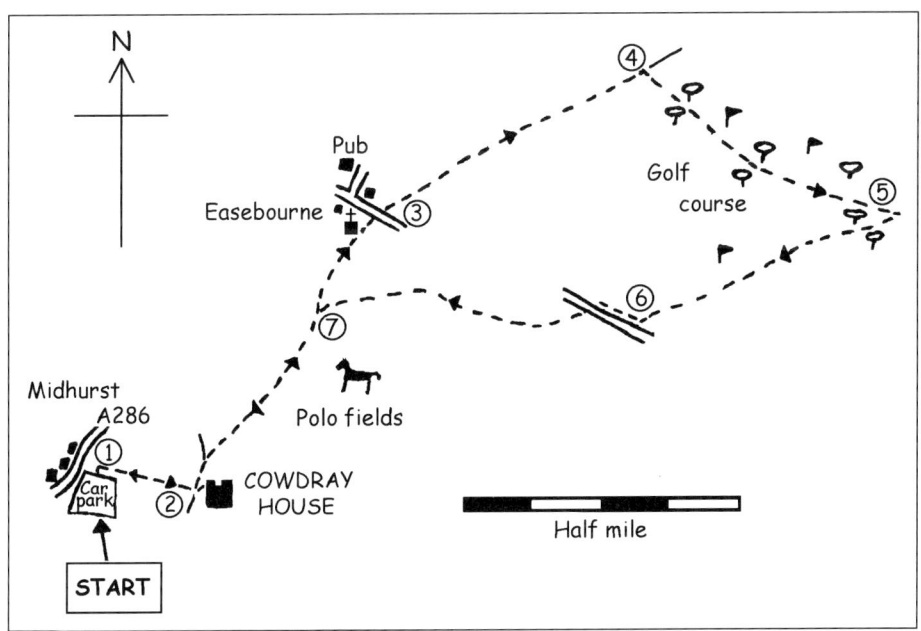

realm. By the end of Henry VIII's reign this arrangement had become formalised and the inner ring, or 'Privy Council', was the real heart of government.

The FitzWilliams had been elevated by Henry VII, and Sir William FitzWilliam became Treasurer to the Royal Household under Henry VIII. This was a key position, involving being in charge of administering the King's personal finances and, as part of the Privy Council, advising him on national policy. As a trusted personal adviser to the King, Sir William was increasingly involved in the delicate negotiations surrounding Henry's attempts to divorce Catherine of Aragon. Sir William was rewarded for this and other services by being made Earl of Southampton and Lord Privy Seal, and as a member of the King's inner circle he played a major part in the overthrow of the increasingly autocratic chief minister, Thomas Cromwell, in 1540.

After Sir William's death his family never regained the same degree of political power, but Cowdray House, the magnificent country home he had developed for himself, continued for many years as a monument to his importance and prestige.

## THE WALK

❶  Leave the car park by a kissing gate in the bottom left-hand corner. Turn right along the path, crossing a bridge to reach a second bridge and gate.

*This path was once the formal drive, leading from estate gates on the edge of Midhurst to Cowdray House, and crossing flood-prone parkland on an embankment.*

Go through the gate to reach the gatehouse of Cowdray House.

*A modest moated manor house had first been built here in 1273 by the local squire, John Bohun. The house and land was bought in 1520 by Sir David Owen, a merchant who had come to prominence with the accession of the Tudors. He pulled down the original house and built a new one in the fashionable quadrangular design, four wings around a central courtyard. The house was bought by Sir William FitzWilliam in 1535 and he received permission to 'crenellate' (fortify) the house. He added the gatehouse and built mock ramparts around the roofline. The fortification was purely for show, since with the end of the Wars of the Roses houses no longer needed to be defensible against anything more than passing thieves.*

*After the death of Sir William, Cowdray House passed to his half-brother Sir Anthony Browne, a rich landowner in his own right, who had acquired the lands of Battle Abbey after the Dissolution in 1538. Browne did not follow his half-brother into politics but instead concentrated upon increasing his fortune as a country gentleman, extending Cowdray House as his family seat. Browne's son, elevated to the peerage as the first Viscount Montague, added the large Tudor windows in 1554, and also the impressive park gates.*

*Although no longer active in national politics, the Montagues remained an important family socially. The young Edward VI visited there in 1552, and Elizabeth I stayed at Cowdray in 1591. The family's fortunes declined in 1605 when the second Viscount Montague was imprisoned for his involvement in the Gunpowder Plot.*

*Legend has it that the last monk to leave Battle Abbey cursed Sir Anthony Browne, predicting that his family would perish by fire and water. In 1793 Cowdray House was gutted by fire and many valuables inside were lost. A few weeks later the eighth Viscount Montague drowned while on holiday in Switzerland, leaving no heirs.*

*The house is today only a ruined shell. Until recently it was open on occasions to the public, but had to be closed. Although there are plans to reopen it eventually, at the time of writing it is closed and can only be viewed from the outside. This is, however, its most imposing aspect.*

❷   After viewing the house, turn left along the tarmac drive. In 150 yards, where the drive bears left, keep straight on, with polo fields on your right. At a cross track in 50 yards, keep ahead through a kissing gate and continue along the track, wooden fence on your right and a hedge on your left. Continue, with the hedge close on your left, and finally with paddocks on your right, to a gate leading onto a lane. Keep ahead along the lane, with houses and Easebourne church on your left, to reach the main road. To visit the White Horse, turn left along the road for 50 yards, and then turn right into a side road. The pub is 50 yards along on your left, just past the village stores.

❸   To continue the walk, cross the road (or turn left if coming from the White Horse) to a track marked 'permissive footpath'. Go through the gate and keep ahead along the track. Cross a stile and continue ahead. The track now narrows to a path and climbs gently between trees.

*This green lane was once a ride along the edge of the parkland that surrounded Cowdray House. To the left you can see a lane: this follows the course of an old road that ran from the village of Easebourne into the surrounding fields and common land from the days of the Normans onwards. Prior to Tudor times, much of the land was common land, where local villagers had for generations had the right to graze their animals, or collect nuts and fruit from the surrounding forest. This provided an essential supplement to their everyday living.*

*Wild deer had roamed the forest, all the property of the King and hunted almost to extinction by Tudor times. Viscount Montague, after the fashion of the new Tudor aristocracy, enclosed his land to create a park, which he stocked with a large herd of deer to provide hunting for himself and his guests. The rights of the ordinary villagers to use the common land and the forest were arbitrarily removed.*

Follow the path for ½ mile, with fine views over the rolling countryside to your left. At the top of the rise, look for a stile on your left. DO NOT cross the stile but instead turn right off the path at a waymark post.

❹   Follow a clear path across the field, climbing towards trees. Go through a gate and continue ahead through a band of trees, to emerge on the golf course. Be aware of flying golf balls on the next part of the walk! Keep straight on across the fairway and drop down through trees to a fingerpost. Keep ahead along the track. Pass a teeing green on your left. Immediately after, DO NOT bear right with the track but keep straight on, with a band of trees on your right (a fingerpost marks the way). Climb to another fingerpost, to the left of a conspicuous tee. Bear half-right, following a line of fingerposts, to cross a fairway and descend into a stand of trees. Enter the trees at a fingerpost and keep ahead along a clear path.

❺   Emerge from the trees and keep ahead along a grassy track for 20 yards to a fingerpost. Here turn sharp right back on yourself and follow another grassy track back through trees, climbing gently to re-emerge on a fairway. Keep ahead across the fairway to a wooden shelter seen opposite. Pass the shelter on your right and walk past the 15th tee to a fingerpost beside a solitary tree ahead. Keep ahead downhill, on the right side of the fairway, parallel to a fence 50 yards off on your left. Aim for a conspicuous oak tree, just to the right of the fairway, with a fingerpost behind.

*The chimneys of Cowdray House can be seen below. The land now covered by the golf course was all part of the deer park in Tudor times. When Queen Elizabeth visited Cowdray in 1591 she hunted in the deer park, where she shot four deer, much to the chagrin of another guest, Lady Kildare, a famed huntress and archer, who only managed to kill one deer.*

From the fingerpost drop down the slope, with the fairway on your left, aiming at two trees seen ahead. Pass between the trees and keep straight on, passing bunkers and a green close on your left, dropping through trees to a sandy track. Turn right to the road.

❻ Go right along the road for 100 yards. At the brow of a hill, carefully cross the road to a footpath sign beside a gate. Go through the gate and half-right down the field, passing a fingerpost in mid-field. Cross a stile and maintain your direction, converging with the corner of a polo field. At the corner turn left and walk, with the fence of the polo field close on your left, to a stile. Maintain direction across a paddock to a stile beside a gate. Cross the stile and turn right to a drive.

❼ Turn left along the drive, with polo fields on your left, and retrace your outward journey to the junction of tracks. Keep ahead to the tarmac drive. Maintain the same direction along the drive to the gates of Cowdray House. Turn right over the bridge and follow the track back to the car park.

# WALK 13
# MICHELHAM PRIORY AND THE DISSOLUTION OF THE MONASTERIES

### Length: 4 miles

*The gatehouse of Michelham Priory*

**HOW TO GET THERE:** Upper Dicker is on the B2108, just south of its junction with the A22 and 3 miles west of Hailsham. The walk starts from the village stores in Upper Dicker.

**PARKING:** There is ample roadside parking in the village, but please park with consideration for the residents.

**MAP:** OS Landranger 199 (GR 552098).

## INTRODUCTION

This pleasant circuit, which is all on the flat and easily walked, starts in the village of Upper Dicker, and goes through fields and woodland that were once part of the estates of the 13th century Michelham Priory. It returns to the priory at the end of the walk, allowing an opportunity to visit (March to October).

## HISTORICAL BACKGROUND

During the Middle Ages the Church was the richest landowner in England after the King, all too often using its spiritual power to protect its secular interests and neglecting its pastoral duties. In the

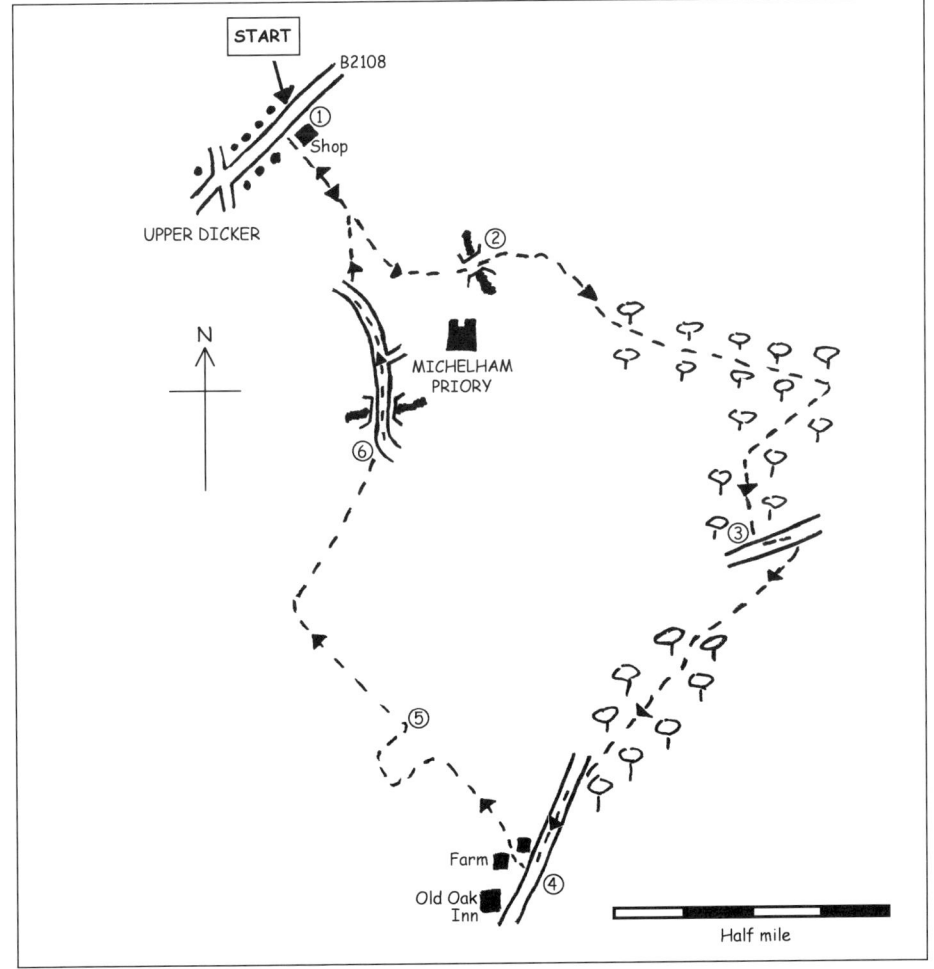

reign of Henry VIII an increasing need to reform the organisation of the Church coincided with the King's political needs, with disastrous results for religious houses such as Michelham Priory.

Henry VIII was a devout Catholic who had been awarded the title of 'Defender of the Faith' by the Pope for his erudite and vigorous defence of Catholicism against the doctrines of Luther. Moreover, despite abuses of power, many religious houses did perform important work helping the poor and needy. Henry had no inclination to join the attack on the Church – known as the Reformation – that was sweeping Northern Europe. However, dynastic considerations were to force his hand.

For most of the previous century, England had been racked by the civil war later known as the Wars of the Roses, as powerful factions vied to control the crown. The reign of Henry's father, Henry VII, had seen several pretenders to the throne inciting rebellion, and Henry VIII's own right to the throne had been contested. Henry was desperate for an heir whose claim would be undisputed, and this meant a son. Although there was no constitutional reason why a queen should not rule England, it was doubted that a woman would be strong enough to rule. Many years of marriage had given Henry only one live child, a daughter Mary, and with no prospect of a son, the spectre of his dynasty being challenged after his death drove Henry to desperate measures. In 1527 he decided to divorce his wife, Queen Catherine of Aragon, and marry the younger Anne Boleyn, who held out the prospect of producing a male child.

Unfortunately for the King, the Pope rejected Henry's ingenious arguments as to why his marriage to Catherine was illegal and refused to grant a divorce. To influence the Pope, Henry started to put pressure on the Church in England, increasingly curbing its powers and attacking its privileges. For five years the Pope resisted Henry's steadily increasing campaign against the Church, until in 1533 he finally excommunicated Henry. The King responded by declaring himself head of the Church in England and the break with Rome was complete. Over the next five years the land and wealth of the Church was subject to widespread confiscation, and in the process known as the Dissolution of the Monasteries most religious houses were closed, their buildings demolished and their monks turned out to fend for themselves.

## THE WALK
N.B. Be prepared for some mud in the woods in point 3.

❶ The village stores are on the south side of the main road through the village (B2108), at the end of a short private road. Facing the shop, go along a footpath to the right of Providence House. Cross the stile and keep straight on to a waymarked stile on the far side of the field. Cross the stile and footbridge and keep straight on across a playing field to a second waymarked stile. After the stile keep straight on, waymarked 'WW', with the hedge on your left, to a fingerpost at a gate. Go through the gate and over a stile in front of the next gate. Bear half-right across the next field, making for a gate to the left of a long barn. Go through the gate, passing the barn on your right, and in 15 yards turn left to a bridge and gate beyond.

*The farm seen today came into being after the Dissolution, and replaced the earlier priory farm. All of the land you are walking across was owned by the priory. There is still a dovecote in the grounds, that provided the monks with meat. One of the feudal rights enjoyed by the priory was that its doves were free to feed on the grain grown by the local peasantry, whilst heavy punishments were imposed upon any peasant who killed one of the priory's doves. The bridge crosses a stream which served a dual function: it fed the moat that protected the priory, and also fishponds which provided fish for the monks.*

❷ Keep ahead, following the track as it bends right over a second bridge. Follow the track, with a hedge on the left, to a gate at the far end.

*The priory can be glimpsed through the trees to the right.*

❸ Cross a stile by the gate and keep straight on, aiming for a stile 20 yards to the left of a gate leading into the woods ahead. Follow the clear path through the trees for ⅓ mile to a gate on the far side of the woods. Go through two gates and turn right along the edge of the field, with the fence close on your right hand. In the bottom corner of the field cross a stile by a gate and turn right along the track. Turn left with the track but then ignore a turn to the right and instead keep ahead along the clear track. Ignore all side turns and follow the track to reach a lane.

**❸**    Turn left along the lane for 70 yards, then, at a horse barrier, turn sharp right into an often muddy bridleway. Follow the bridleway, keeping the woods on your left. After ¼ mile, keep ahead into trees. Cross a bridge and continue along the track to reach a lane (this track is often very muddy but can be avoided by using parallel paths on the left). Turn left along the lane for 400 yards, to reach the drive to Primrose Farm on your right.

**❹**    The Old Oak Inn is a further 100 yards along the lane. To continue the walk, turn into the drive of Primrose Farm. Although currently unmarked, a public footpath goes through the farmyard. Follow the concrete drive rightwards through the farm buildings and then on between fields. Turn right and then left with the track, now unsurfaced. Follow the track around three sides of a large field (the right of way crosses the field, but there is no evidence of it on the ground, and the farmer expects the track to be used instead).

**❺**    At a gate on the far side of the field, by a water cistern, turn left with the track across a field towards woods. Go beneath power cables to a gate. Once through the gate, keep straight on with the track across the next field. On the far side of the field, by a telegraph pole, DO NOT go ahead through the gate and over the culvert. Instead turn right along a cross-track for 5 yards and then turn left over a plank bridge and a stile into the field. Follow a path across the field, passing just to the left of a telegraph pole and aiming at a white post in the hedge ahead. At the white waymark post turn left and walk along the field boundary. Follow the grassy track through two fields. In the third field diverge from the track and aim for a stile 20 yards to the left of the gate ahead.

**❻**    Cross the stile onto a road and turn left. Follow the road over a bridge and to the gates of Michelham Priory. It is open from March to October on Wednesday to Sunday, 10.30 am to dusk. There is an admission charge.

*Michelham Priory was built in 1229 for the Augustinian order by local landowner Gilbert de Aquila. He built the priory on the site of one of his manor houses, and gave the attached estate to the priory for its upkeep. As an additional income he also made over to the priory a number of the feudal rights of his various estates, such as the right to graze pigs in the distant Ashdown Forest. In return for his beneficence, the monks of Michelham were expected to say daily prayers for de Aquila, and continue with masses on his behalf after his death.*

*Michelham was poorly run as a religious house. The monks did not take their religious duties seriously,*

**REFRESHMENTS**

Upper Dicker has a pub and a shop. The walk also passes close to the Old Oak Inn, an attractive and award-winning country pub offering bar food, with curries a speciality, guest beers and a beer garden (telephone: 01323 482072).

*and fines were levied by the Church authorities on its monks for absenting themselves from the priory without good reason, for breaking their vows of silence and for visiting local taverns. Successive priors were more concerned with their duties as feudal landlords than with being pastors to their congregation, and used their ecclesiastical power to protect and maximize their secular income. The resentment thus caused made the priory a target for the Peasants' Revolt in 1381, after which the massive gatehouse seen today was built to protect the priory from its parishioners. A moat was dug as an extra defence.*

*In 1538 the priory was dissolved, its monks turned out and much of its land auctioned off. Many of its buildings were pulled down, the lead from the roof and glass from the windows sold, and the stones used by local farmers. A mansion was built out of the south range of the priory, and gardens were laid out where the church had stood. The gatehouse was retained, and a large portion of the land was kept in order to provide the basis of an affluent farmstead.*

*Today Michelham Priory is owned by Sussex Archeological Trust, and houses a collection of furniture, tapestries, toys, and musical instruments, as well as brass rubbings and paintings.*

After viewing the priory, continue along the road for a further 200 yards, then turn right across the gates to Oldwaye, to a stile beside a gate. Cross the stile and keep straight on to a telegraph pole, and then continue ahead to a stile into the sports field of St Bedes School. Retrace your outward steps across the sports field and the field beyond, back into Upper Dicker.

# WALK **14**

# ARUNDEL CASTLE AND THE ELIZABETHAN COLD WAR

## Length: 3½ miles

*Arundel Castle*

**HOW TO GET THERE:** The walk starts from the Black Rabbit public house on a minor road that passes the eastern side of Arundel Castle and continues to the hamlet of Offham. This road leads off a roundabout reached just after crossing the river into Arundel, if approaching the town from the A27.

**PARKING:** There is a small public car park beside the pub. Alternatively, there is a large pay-and-display car park (passed on the walk) opposite the castle gates, 50 yards along the minor road to Offham. This is recommended at peak periods.

**MAPS:** OS Landranger 197 (GR 025085).

## INTRODUCTION

This easy stroll includes a delightful stretch beside the River Arun, approaching Arundel along water meadows and offering the most spectacular views of Arundel Castle. The route passes the front of the castle itself and then goes round the lovely Swanbourne Lake in the historic deer park.

## HISTORICAL BACKGROUND

The reign of Queen Elizabeth I saw increasing conflict between Protestants and Catholics in England, and the Fitzalans and the Howards of Arundel Castle were at the heart of that conflict.

The Reformation had divided Europe into two camps ideologi-

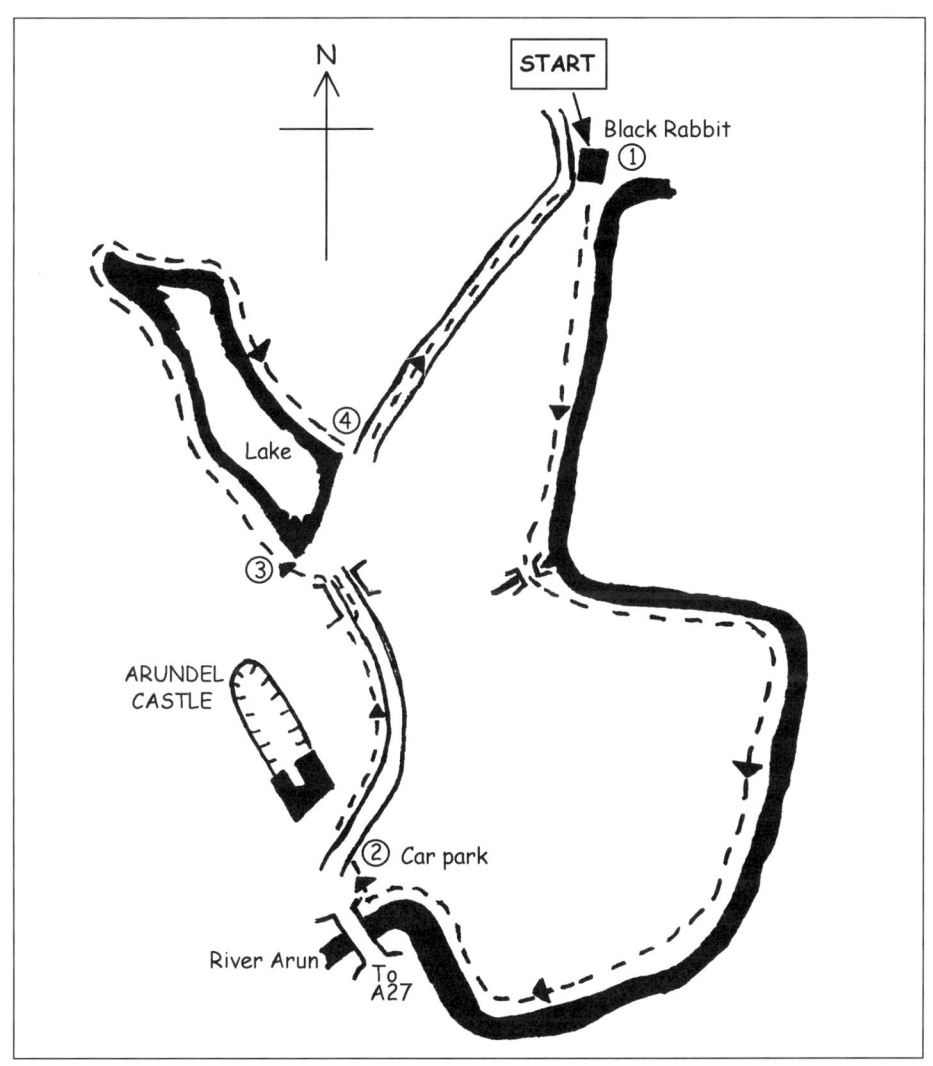

cally, and religion became the cause of, or at least a veneer upon, many of the conflicts between and within nations. The introduction of the Reformation into England by Henry VIII had been primarily for political and dynastic reasons, and Henry was content to accept a public display of loyalty from his subjects whilst turning a blind eye to continued Catholic worship in private. His daughter Elizabeth I initially continued this tolerant policy. An outward show of conformity to the new religion was required, and church-going, especially amongst men of substance, was enforced. Public endorsement of Catholicism was liable to fines and imprisonment, although in private men were allowed to a large degree to obey their consciences, so long as this was done discreetly. A third of the English nobility remained Catholic, as did a sizeable percentage of the gentry.

Henry Fitzalan, 12th Earl of Arundel, had been a leading supporter of Elizabeth's sister and predecessor, the Catholic Queen Mary, and was rewarded with the influential office of Lord Steward of the Royal Household. He had married into the powerful Percy family, Catholics and effective rulers of northern England, and his son-in-law was Thomas Howard, Duke of Norfolk, England's only duke and the leading Catholic in the land. Upon her accession in 1558, Elizabeth, who could not afford to offend her Catholic lords, kept Fitzalan in office, but never trusted him.

By 1570 England had become the foremost of the Protestant countries of northern Europe. The Catholic powers, led by Spain, were determined to destabilise England and replace Elizabeth with a suitably Catholic monarch, namely her cousin Mary, Queen of Scots. English Catholics were seen as tools in this cold war. In 1572 a conspiracy, known as the Ridolfi Plot, to assassinate Elizabeth and replace her with Mary was uncovered. The Duke of Norfolk was implicated, together with his father-in-law, Fitzalan of Arundel. Both were tried and executed for treason.

Fitzalan's estates passed to Norfolk's son-in-law, the 15 year old Philip Howard. Despite his strong Catholic credentials – both his father and his grandfather having died for the Catholic cause and his godfather being no less than King Philip of Spain – young Philip showed no interest in religion or politics. After a period of probation, Philip was soon accepted in Elizabeth's court as a lively, extravagant and above all non-political courtier, and in 1580 was rewarded by being granted his grandfather's title, Earl of Arundel.

However, Philip Howard's political innocence was soon to end. Through his openly Catholic wife Anne, Philip became implicated in the Throckmorton Plot, another plot to replace Elizabeth with Mary, Queen of Scots. Philip was arrested and subjected to severe interrogation. This experience forced him to re-evalue his beliefs and lifestyle. In 1584 he retired from court to Arundel Castle and became a Catholic. He initially thought that, hidden away in Sussex, he could keep his conversion a secret, but the strain became too great and in 1585 he sneaked to the nearby port of Littlehampton and attempted to flee to France. His ship was boarded just offshore, and Howard was arrested and imprisoned in the Tower. After the Spanish attempt to invade England with the Armada in 1588, Howard was feared to be a potential focus for Catholic opposition to the Queen, and was tried for treason on the grounds of being a Catholic and attempting to leave the country without permission. Howard now stood by his new-found faith, and was imprisoned in the Tower for the rest of his life. He died in prison in 1595. Nearly four centuries later, Philip Howard was canonised by Pope Paul VI as a martyr to his faith.

## THE WALK

❶ **If starting from the Black Rabbit**, from the back of the public car park beside the pub, go onto the river bank and walk along, with the river on your left, towards Arundel Castle seen in the distance. In ½ mile, ignore paths going right, but cross a sluice gate and continue along the river. Continue for a further 1¼ miles, until reaching a car park on your right. Follow the path between the car park and tea garden to reach the ruins of Blackfriars.

*The ruins of Blackfriars are all that remain of a small Dominican 'Maison Dieu', or hospice, founded in the 13th century by Isobel, Countess of Arundel. The hospice was permanent home to 20 men of the parish, 'aged or infirm but of good life', and was administered by Dominican monks, whose other duties included caring for travellers, of which there were many. The bridge at Arundel was the lowest crossing point of the river, and downstream of it was a small port marking the highest point coastal vessels could reach. Arundel was thus a bustling crossroads for merchants and travellers.*

*When Henry VIII took England out of the Catholic faith, the wealth of the church was seized in the process known as the Dissolution of the*

*Monasteries. Arundel Priory was disbanded at that time and its land was bought in 1538 by the Earl of Arundel.*

❷    Cross the road to the gatehouse of the castle. (**If starting from the long stay car park, start here.**) The privately owned castle is open from 1st April until 31st October, Monday to Saturday, noon to 5 pm. It is possible to visit the gardens separately from the castle. There is an admission charge.

*The first castle at Arundel was begun in 1070 by Roger de Montgomery, to defend the strategically important point where a gap through the South Downs coincided with a river crossing. The Norman arch and walls of the inner gateway date from this time, and the original Norman 'motte', or raised earthen mound upon which the keep was built, can still be seen.*

*The castle was besieged and captured by Henry I in 1102, when its owner sided with the Duke of Normandy against the King. In 1135 the small castle was given to Queen Adela, widow of Henry I, whose second husband William of Albini was created Earl de Arundel. During the 16 year long civil war in the 12th century, when the throne was disputed between Stephen and his cousin Matilda, William was a supporter of Queen Matilda, and Arundel successfully withstood a second siege by Stephen's army in 1139.*

*In 1243 the male Albini line died out, and Arundel castle passed through the female line into the up-and-coming Fitzalan family. The Fitzalan earls reinforced the castle, building the outer barbican, strengthening the keep and raising the walls. Arundel Castle remained the home of the Fitzalan Earls of Arundel until Henry, 12th Earl, was executed in 1572 for his involvement in the Ridolfi Plot to assassinate the Queen. The castle and estates passed through Henry's daughter Mary into the Howard family, where it has remained ever since.*

*During the Civil War the Duke of Norfolk fought on the side of the King, and in 1644 Arundel Castle was besieged for a third time, by Parliamentarian forces. The garrison held out for eighteen days before surrendering. To prevent it being used again, the castle was 'slighted' – its walls torn down and the keep and gatehouse destroyed.*

*Arundel Castle remained a ruin for nearly 150 years until the 8th Duke started to restore it in 1716. Restoration continued off and on until 1903. Most of the structure that can be seen today is Victorian, but the original Norman undercroft still survives beneath the Great Hall and the Well Tower is basically 13th century.*

To continue the walk, follow the path along the left side of the road, next to the ornamental castle moat, with fine close-up views of the castle to your left. Where the path ends, continue along the side of the road for a few yards and go over a bridge. Just 10 yards after the bridge, turn left on to a marked footpath and go through a squeeze stile into Arundel Park.

> **REFRESHMENTS**
>
> The Black Rabbit has large terraces fronting onto the river, with riverside beer gardens and a children's play area. It offers a wide range of food (telephone: 01903 882828). There are also many pubs, tearooms and shops in Arundel itself.

❸ Follow the path along the side of the lake.

*The lake was originally the water supply for a Saxon mill pond, mentioned in the Domesday Book. It later became the water supply for the castle. The lake was painted by John Constable.*

At the end of the lake, do not cross a stile ahead into the park, but instead turn right and follow the main track, continuing around the lake.

*The park was originally enclosed in Tudor times by the Fitzalan earls as a deer park. Hunting deer was a favourite pastime amongst the gentry in Tudor England, and it was usual for great landowners to enclose areas of their estates and stock them with deer herds, to provide sport for themselves and visitors.*

Follow the lake shore back to a kiosk and lodge.

❹ Go out of the park onto the road. Turn left and follow the quiet road for ½ mile to reach the Black Rabbit public house.

# WALK 15

# HASTINGS AND ORGANISED CRIME IN THE 18TH CENTURY

**Length: 4½ miles**

*Net houses in Hastings*

**HOW TO GET THERE:** Hastings is on the A21, 5 miles east of Bexhill. The walk starts at the Dolphin Inn, on Hastings seafront next to the net houses.

**PARKING:** The Rock A Nore pay-and-display car park is almost next to the Dolphin; there are several other car parks in the town.

**MAP:** OS Landranger 199 (GR 827092).

## INTRODUCTION

This splendid walk starts in the heart of the historic old town of Hastings, and then goes along the cliffs to Fairlight Glen, one of the favourite landing spots for 18th century smugglers, particularly the notorious Mayfield Gang. There are stunning views from the cliffs and pleasant stretches through woods on the return journey. This circuit involves some fairly strenuous ups and downs, but route finding throughout is easy.

## HISTORICAL BACKGROUND

Hastings was at the heart of a key industry in the 18th century, smuggling. During that time illegal trade mushroomed, and what had previously been small-scale evasion of duty turned into an industry of huge proportions. The reason for this was simple: throughout the previous century, successive governments had levied ever higher taxes to pay for foreign wars. To the long established 'customs' duty, levied upon imports, was added the new 'excise' duty, a tax upon consumption. All manner of goods were subject to taxation, commodities such as wool, silks, tea and chocolate as well as tobacco and spirits. Legitimate merchants were happy to buy tax-free goods on the black market, fuelling a growth industry.

Traditionally, many of England's seamen, be they fishermen, colliers, or crews of coastal vessels, had used their skills in navigation to sneak a few illicit items into the country, but by the mid-18th century this private enterprise had become organised crime. Wealthy merchants and financiers, well-connected socially and politically, would provide venture capital, which was used by middlemen to buy

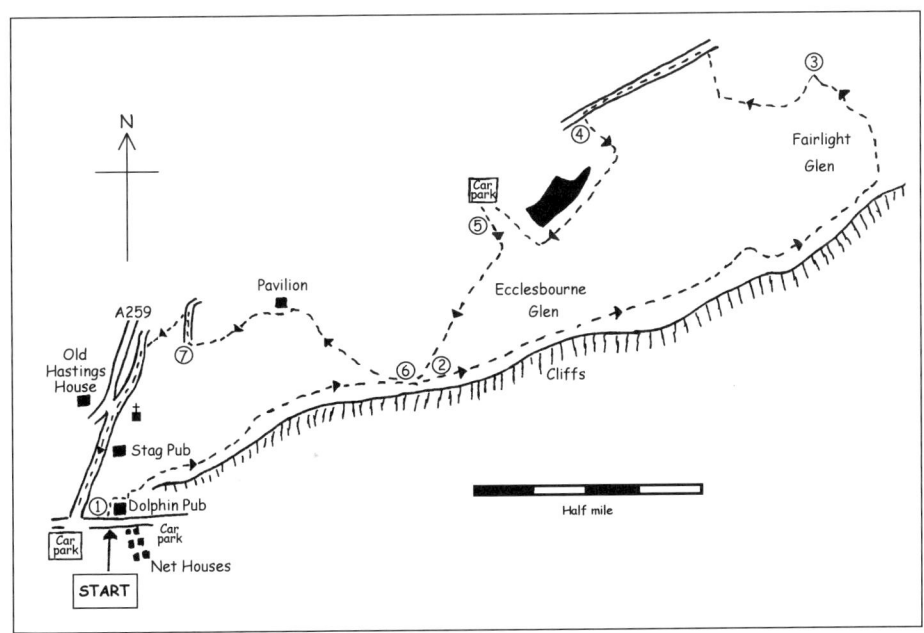

goods on the Continent. These middlemen would contract shipowners to get the contraband into England, and the shipowners in turn would hire local seamen to run the cargoes across the Channel. Once on the English coast, the contraband would be discreetly landed on deserted beaches and coves, where whole communities would connive at their transportation inland.

Profit margins were huge. Brandy or tobacco would sell in England at four times its purchase price in France or Holland, tea would sell at eight times its purchase price. Initially these transactions would be paid for in cash, but as smuggling became ever more organised, it was simpler for English merchants to buy their contraband by banker's draft, so blatant was the trade.

As smuggling increased, so did Government attempts to clamp down, but the problems facing them were huge. Smuggling gangs were large and well-armed, frequently outnumbering the revenue officers sent to intercept them, and they did not hesitate to use considerable violence to evade arrest. With whole communities abetting the smugglers, either for reward or through intimidation, getting information about the trade was difficult. Even when evidence was found, local dignitaries such as the squire or the magistrate were frequently bought off by the gangs. Such was the political, social and economic power of the rich backers of smuggling that effective legislation was impossible, and organised crime flourished largely unchecked throughout the 18th century.

## THE WALK

❶   With your back to the net houses, and facing the Dolphin Inn, climb up Tamarisk Steps to the left of the pub. Turn right with the steps and climb to the viewpoint.

*The tall timber net houses, unique in Britain, were introduced in Tudor times to store nets and fishing tackle, and were also used as a temporary hiding place for contraband by 18th century smugglers. Their odd shape is due to the desire to occupy as little ground area as possible, and thereby reduce the land tax that had to be paid. Fishing took place directly from the open beach, called the Stade, in front of these buildings.*

Turn left up the street for 20 yards and then turn right up more steps to reach the top station of the funicular railway. Turn right again and climb more steps to reach an open green sward.

*The Hastings we see today is largely due to expansion over the last 150 years. In the 18th century the town was much smaller and clustered between this hill and the hill opposite, crowned with the castle. The old town was fronted by the Stade, the economic heart of Hastings. Smuggling was an essential part of the local economy, and much contraband was landed directly onto the beach. The town's population, fully aware of the trade and seeing nothing immoral in avoiding customs duties, abetted the smugglers. Revenue officers or 'excisemen', totally outnumbered, were either bribed or intimidated into making themselves scarce when illicit cargoes were being landed, although occasionally they would seize part of a cargo, with the agreement of the smugglers, in order to demonstrate that they were doing their job.*

*Such was the popular sympathy for the smugglers that as late as 1821 an exciseman, George England, was convicted of murder by a local jury after he had accidentally shot a local fisherman-cum-smuggler who had refused to have his boat searched. When the Government intervened to reprieve England there were riots in Hastings, so serious that troops had to be sent in to restore order.*

From the top of the steps turn right, in the direction signed 'cliff walks'. Walk with the cliff close on your right hand for ½ mile to reach a kissing gate.

❷    Go through the kissing gate and descend steps to the right, to Ecclesbourne Glen.

*Although small cargoes of contraband were blatantly brought into Hastings itself, the really large cargoes were landed at the more secluded coves, such as Ecclesbourne and Fairlight, further along the coast. Most landings were at night, from large specially built black-painted vessels, rigged fore and aft to enable them to sail into any anchorage, whatever the wind. Lanterns and beacons on the cliffs would guide the ships to land. It was not unusual for 3,000 gallons of spirits to be brought in on a single trip.*

*Speed of unloading was of the essence, and such was their organisation that smugglers could muster hundreds of local labourers within hours, to be synchronised with landings. In the 18th century there was crushing rural poverty, with low wages and high unemployment. One fifth of the population of Sussex received 'parish relief', a subsistence level handout from the state, whilst for those who could get work, a week's backbreaking labour in the fields would earn seven shillings. The same could be earned in a single night by 'moonlighting', unloading for the smugglers.*

Continue by going up steps, direction 'Fairlight Glen', and then walk along the clifftop for ¾ mile. Where there is a choice of paths, stay right, i.e., closest to the cliff. Finally descend steps to Fairlight Glen. At the bottom of the steps turn left along a broad path, with the beach down to your right through the trees.

*Fairlight Glen was a popular destination for smugglers in the 18th century. Smuggling in Sussex was mostly controlled by large inland gangs operating out of Hawkhurst, Goudhurst and Mayfield. Fairlight Glen was the favoured landing spot of the Mayfield Gang, led at the start of the century by one Gabriel Tompkins but backed by many eminent citizens who gave financial and political support. Tompkins could assemble up to 500 men for one night's work. Local labour would be recruited to carry goods up the steep path to teams of pack mules waiting on the cliffs above. 'Bat men', muscular thugs armed with clubs, would be posted to protect the operation from any interference, but usually bribery combined with the threat of violence were enough to ensure that revenue officers stayed away.*

*Smugglers used the coves at Fairlight Glen to land their booty*

*Tompkins was eventually convicted for smuggling and murder. To escape sentence he turned in a number of former colleagues and corrupt revenue officers, and was rewarded by being appointed a bailiff for the Sheriff of Sussex. Over the next few years he arrested numerous local smugglers. Despite his defection, the Mayfield Gang, under new leadership, continued to flourish. Tompkins himself finally turned to highway robbery, for which he was hanged in 1750.*

Follow the path as it climbs again, curving leftwards and upwards. Ignore steps climbing up to the right but continue with the path until it flattens out. Walk along to a junction of tracks at an information board, at the top of Fairlight Glen.

*The steep path on the left was the route by which the smugglers would bring up their goods from the beach to the teams of pack mules waiting above. So organised and quasi-legitimate was the trade that special packaging was designed for the contraband by Continental retailers. For instance, a standard hogshead of wine, holding 140 gallons, was impossible to conceal or carry up a cliff at dead of night, so wine was decanted into manageable 4 gallon barrels before shipping. Additionally, barrels were made with flattened sides so that two could conveniently be worn in a harness and carried by one man. Similarly, tea and tobacco were sent over in small waterproof bundles.*

❸  DO NOT go through the kissing gate on your right, nor drop sharp left down into the glen. Instead go half-left, climbing slightly. Follow the path as it levels out and goes along the side of a field to a track. Pass through a metal barrier and keep ahead along the track, signed 'Barley Lane'. Ignore a field gate to the right.

*From here contraband, now on the backs of the mules, was moved inland to places such as Mayfield and Hawkhurst, where it was repackaged by legitimate merchants before being moved to its final retail markets in London and the Midlands. Vast convoys, with up to 150 men and 300 horses, would move the goods, whilst the local population wisely stayed beneath the bedclothes.*

On reaching the lane turn left for ¼ mile, passing cottages on your left.

❹    Pass through a metal gate, ignoring a footpath to Ore on the right. Turn left along a track, signed 'No entry except for access'. In 40 yards, at a gate to 'Fishponds Farmhouse', bear right through a kissing gate. Keep ahead and follow a clear path into woods. Follow the path as it descends, curving left and then right. After 250 yards, ignore a left turn but continue slightly downhill on the main path. Stay on the main path, ignoring side turns uphill, until you pass a reservoir on your right. About 200 yards past the end of the reservoir, at a junction of paths at a bollard, turn right up steps. Follow the path past a caravan site and out to a car park. DO NOT cross the car park, but turn left along the bottom fence and out through a barrier near the bottom left corner.

❺    Follow the path as it swings parallel to the coast, with fine views opening up. Keep ahead, ignoring paths to both right and left, to go through a kissing gate after nearly ½ mile and regain the coast path.

❻    DO NOT follow the fence on your left hand but bear right up the slope to emerge on a grassy sward. Go diagonally across the grass, veering away from the sea. Eventually a sports pavilion comes into view ahead. Pass the pavilion on your right hand and follow the hedge. At a fingerpost in 20 yards descend right. Continue down the right-hand side of a grassy area. In the bottom corner turn right and follow a path to emerge at the end of a road.

❼    Follow the road, with houses on your right. Where the road bends right, bear left down steps, with a railing on your left. In 15 yards, turn left down more steps and keep ahead down a tarmac path to reach the road. Turn left along the road to reach All Saints' church.

*Smuggling flourished because it had at least the tacit support of the local population. Defrauding the revenue, rather than being viewed as a crime, was seen as laudable. Popular support evaporated in the 1760s, however, when local smugglers overstepped the mark. A notorious band of local smugglers known as Ruxley's Crew turned from running contraband to piracy. They would board ships off the coast, lock the crew below deck, steal the cargo and then scupper the ship with all hands. When Ruxley bragged around the taverns of Hastings of his brutal murder of a Dutch sea captain he caused public revulsion. He was denounced from the pulpit of All Saints' church, a public enquiry into smuggling activities was* demanded, and the Mayor was attacked by outraged citizens when he failed to condemn the gang. As a direct consequence troops were posted in Hastings and a man-of-war patrolled the coast, and the gang were arrested. Despite the public revulsion of him, no local jury dare convict Ruxley, and he and his men were sent to London for trial.

    On the opposite side of London Road is Old Hastings House, the Georgian red brick building with a white arch facing the church. This was home to John Collier, Mayor of Hastings in 1735 and one of the chief opponents of smuggling. Lacking public support at that time, his success in combating the trade was limited.

> **REFRESHMENTS**
>
> There are numerous pubs in Hastings, many with smuggling connections. One passed near the end of the walk is the Stag Inn, an 18th century smugglers' haunt, with dark oak beams and a tiered beer garden. It offers a good range of beers and food, especially ploughman's lunches (telephone: 01424 425734). There are also numerous shops and cafés in Hastings.

Continue past the church. Walk down All Saints Street, passing the Stag public house on your left.

*The Stag Inn was a favourite haunt of smugglers in the 18th century. Its cellars were once connected by tunnels to the cliffs above, and contraband was hidden here. All Saints Street was one of the main thoroughfares in Old Hastings, and is still lined with many fascinating old buildings.*

At the seafront, turn left back to the car park by the Dolphin Inn.

*Throughout the 18th century smuggling flourished, and all attempts to control it foundered. Even the onset of the Napoleonic Wars and the imposition of a blockade upon Europe failed to halt the flow of contraband across the Channel. Eventually it was economics not politics that brought smuggling to an end. In the 1840s Britain adopted free trade, and slashed import duties. The merchants and bankers who had funded the organised crime could now make their profits legally, and large-scale smuggling, starved of funds, gradually withered away.*

# WALK 16

# BALCOMBE VIADUCT
# AND THE GOLDEN AGE OF RAIL

### Length: 7½ miles

*Balcombe Viaduct, one of the wonders of the Victorian Age*

**HOW TO GET THERE:**
Balcombe is midway between Crawley and Haywards Heath, on the B2036 Cuckfield to Crawley road.

**PARKING:** There is free parking in a large layby on the B2036, just north of the village. Drive out of Balcombe, passing the church on the right and the 'B2110 Handcross' junction on the left; the layby is on the right, immediately past the derestriction sign.

**MAP:** OS Landranger 187 (GR 307310).

## INTRODUCTION

This walk starts in the village of Balcombe, goes through parkland and woods and then along the banks of the delightful Ardingly Reservoir. It then continues to Balcombe Viaduct, regarded as one of the wonders of the railway age, before returning across fields and through woods to Balcombe. Although undulating, this walk has no steep gradients but it can be muddy in places.

## HISTORICAL BACKGROUND

In the mid-19th century Britain was the leading commercial nation in the world, a position that owed much to the genius of its industrial and civil engineers. One of the most enduring monuments to that genius in Sussex is Balcombe Viaduct.

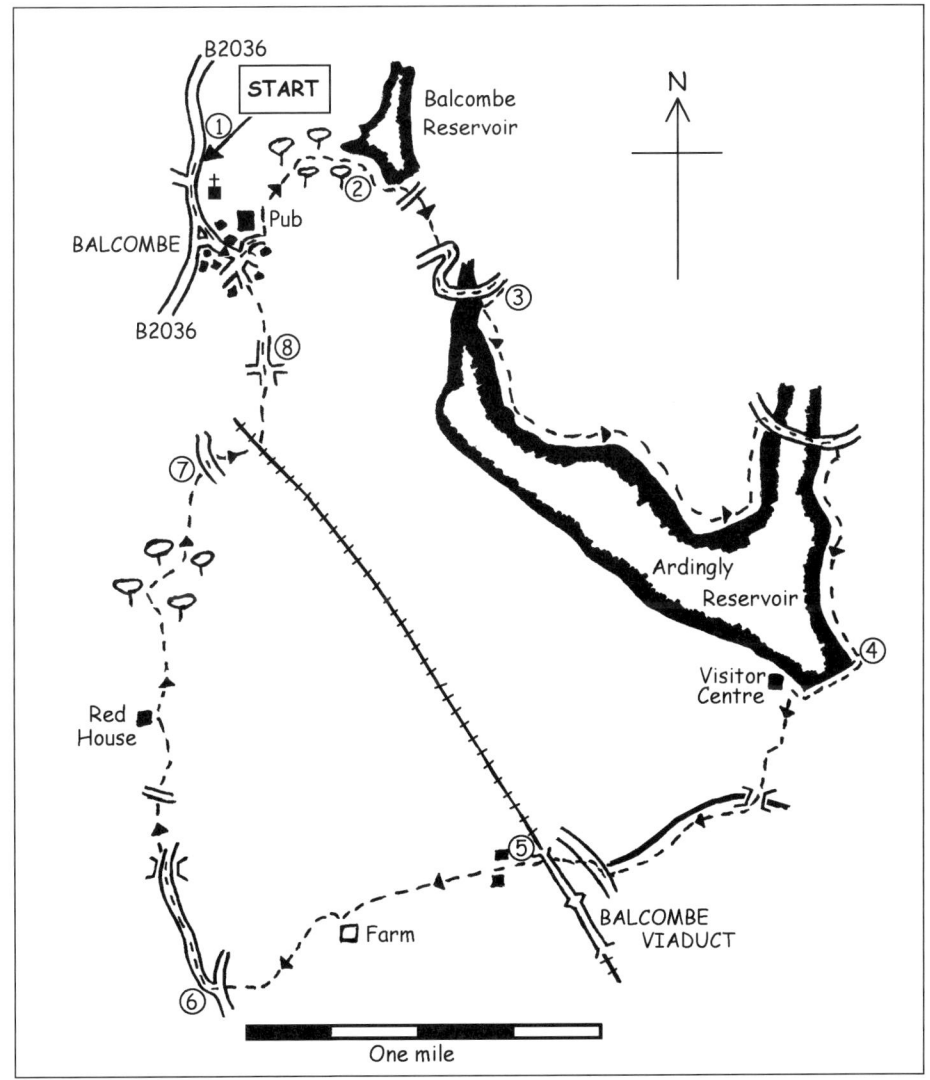

The most obvious reason for Britain's commercial superiority in the mid-19th century was that industrialisation had taken place earlier in Britain than elsewhere, giving British manufacturers a lead over other nations that was not challenged until the end of the century. The Industrial Revolution could not have happened, however, without a corresponding revolution in transport. Large-scale production needed not only new technology and new ways of organising labour, but also the means to move increasing quantities of raw materials and finished goods quickly and cheaply around the country. In the mid-18th century these means did not exist.

The revolution in transport began in 1759, with the building of the first commercial canal, and for 60 years canals were opened the length and breadth of Britain. But canal transport was slow, and there were physical limitations upon where they could be built, and alternatives were sought. Tramways, iron rails along which laden wagons were pulled by horses, had existed in the coalfields for decades, and by 1800 horse-power was replaced by stationary steam engines winching the wagons along. The obvious next step was for the engine itself to be mobile, and the search was on to design the first 'locomotive'. Enter George Stephenson, greatest of the early railway pioneers.

Stephenson started out as a cowherd and colliery labourer, illiterate until he was 20, but with a natural genius for all things mechanical. Between 1816 and 1822 Stephenson built a number of prototype steam locomotives, but the breakthrough came in 1825 when he designed and built a railway to carry coal from Darlington to the river port of Stockton. As well as coal, the Stockton-Darlington railway carried passengers. Four years later, Liverpool and Manchester were linked by a much larger scale railway, which generated huge profits and encouraged the development of railways all over the country. The age of the railway had arrived.

## THE WALK

❶   From the layby, walk up the hill, passing the church on your left. Turn left at the green, opposite the school, into Haywards Heath Road. Continue to a crossroads, with the Half Moon pub on the corner. Turn left, with the pub on your left hand, and walk along the cul-de-sac, passing the village stores. Turn right with a tarmac drive. Just after the last house on the right, turn left through a kissing gate, beside a field gate, and proceed down the left side of the field.

*You are entering Balcombe Park, formerly the grounds of Highley Manor and laid out in the 14th century as a deer park by the Duke of Norfolk. Highley Manor has subsequently been demolished. The large Georgian house on your left is Balcombe House, formerly the village rectory.*

Continue down the field to reach a kissing gate leading into woods. Follow the path down through the trees for 100 yards, to a junction at a fingerpost. Turn right and follow the main path across several plank bridges. Continue along an open area and back into trees. Soon Balcombe Reservoir comes into view.

*Despite appearances to the contrary, Balcombe Reservoir is man-made, intended as a fishing lake for Highley Manor.*

❷   Follow the banks of the reservoir to a kissing gate into a field. Keep straight on along the bottom of the field and turn left over a footbridge and through a kissing gate. Go half left across the next field to a kissing gate into a lane. Cross the lane to a stile and go along the left edge of the field to another stile. Keep in the same direction across the next field and down through trees to a lane. Turn left along the lane for 350 yards to cross the head of Ardingly Reservoir. Climb with the road for 200 yards, then turn right through a gate (a layby is opposite).

❸   Descend the path to the shore of the reservoir. Follow the lakeside shore for 1½ miles to reach a road. Turn right and cross the lake on a causeway. At the far end of the causeway turn right through a kissing gate and resume the lakeside path. Walk alongside the lake for a further ⅔ mile, ignoring turnings to the left, to emerge on the dam.

*This is Ardingly Reservoir, created in 1978 when the dam was constructed to flood 78 hectares of land. The water is used to top up the River Ouse in times of drought.*

❹   Cross the dam, passing the visitors centre (toilets and snacks) on the right. Climb the grass bank to the side of the drive to the Disabled Car Park, aiming at a clearly visible fingerpost. At the top of the bank, DO NOT go to the fingerpost but turn half-left with the grassy track. Go through a kissing gate and along the left-hand side of a field. Follow the fence to a gap in the hedge. Go through the gap and turn left down the field boundary.

*Balcombe Viaduct is visible to the right. The viaduct was necessary to carry the track on a level course across the valley of the Ouse, which divides the Weald from the Downs.*

Cross a plank bridge and keep ahead to another, more substantial bridge. Cross this and turn right along the bank of the Ouse for ½ mile to reach the road. Turn right across the bridge. Go along the road for 80 yards and then, opposite a white cottage, turn left through a gate. Go half-right to the last-but-one arch of the viaduct.

*The first railways were all built by private companies, with money provided by large and small investors who saw in the new technology the opportunity for quick riches. Throughout the 1830s and 1840s railways spread like a rash across Britain, with huge numbers of individual companies rushing to build railways, often in competition with another line close by and all too often with scant regard for the commercial viability of their scheme. Over 13,000 miles of track were built in this period of 'railway mania'.*

*The London & Brighton Railway Company was launched to link the growing resort of Brighton to the capital. Unlike many railway schemes, there was sound commercial reasoning behind this one, and the completion of the line in 1842 ensured Brighton's place as one of England's leading holiday destinations.*

*Balcombe Viaduct was an essential link in the London to Brighton Railway. The viaduct was designed in 1842 by John Urpeth Rastrick, a largely self-taught civil engineer. His 37 brick arches carried the track for 1,475 feet across the valley, 80 feet up at the highest. The viaduct was the most ambitious piece of railway engineering in Sussex, also one of the longest viaducts in England, and the owners of the company wished it to be visually pleasing as well as functional. Caen limestone was imported to face the brickwork, and architect David Moccata was employed to add aesthetic touches such as the classical balustrade and the mock Grecian pagodas on each end.*

❺ Go under the viaduct and keep ahead to a stile beside a link fence. Follow the path, which can be overgrown in summer, to a second stile into a field. Maintain direction across the field to a fingerpost and stile, then turn left down a track. Continue rightwards between buildings and then turn left through a gate at a fingerpost. Follow the right-hand boundary of the field to a double stile just below the top right-hand corner. Cross the stile and go half-left down the next field, aiming for a large tree in the far corner. Go over a stile into the next field and follow the right-hand edge towards a bridge. Cross the bridge and go half-right across the field, following the telegraph poles, to pick up the hedge on the left-hand side. Follow the hedge to the far end of the long field, ignoring a gate on the left leading up to a farm, to reach steps at the far end. Climb onto a track and turn right. Follow the track for ½ mile to a road.

❻ Cross the road half left into Cherry Lane. Follow the lane for 500 yards to an inconspicuous railed bridge. Cross the bridge and immediately go through a gateway on the left, at a fingerpost. Turn right and go up the left-hand field boundary, aiming past a telegraph pole to a red house seen on the skyline. At the top of the bank climb steps to a fingerpost. Cross half-left over a lane to a fingerpost and stile. Go up the field to a stile behind a tree immediately ahead. Cross the next small field to a stile by a tree. Follow the left-hand boundary of the third and then the fourth fields, always maintaining the same direction. Eventually reach a track in the far corner of the field. Follow the track down to a T-junction. Cross over and keep straight on down into woods, bearing right at a fingerpost in 20 yards. Follow the clearly waymarked path down through woods to a stile leading into a field. Go half-left up the field to a stile, to the left of a clump of trees. Cross the stile and follow an enclosed footpath out to a road.

❼ Turn left up the road for 50 yards and then turn right at a fingerpost up a drive. Continue past an ex-farm on the right and Kemps House on the left. At the end of the drive take a footpath to the right, leading to the railway. Cross the busy line with care, and follow an enclosed footpath to a stile into a field. Walk along the right-hand edge of the field, with the hedge close on your right. Follow the footpath, passing to the right of a red-brick house, out to a road.

❽ Keep ahead along 'Jobes' opposite. Where the road bends left, keep straight on along the footpath, first past houses and then along the side of a recreation field. Continue along the footpath to a road.

Turn left along the road to a T-junction, where you turn right back to the Half Moon Inn. Turn left just before the pub in Haywards Heath Road and retrace your outward steps back to the start.

**REFRESHMENTS**

There are pubs, shops and a tearoom in Balcombe, and a snack-bar at Ardingly Reservoir. The Half Moon pub in Balcombe is walker-friendly, with flagstone floors, dark oak beams and a range of food (telephone: 01444 811582).

*The railway bubble burst in 1847.*
*For two decades a mood of semi-hysteria had gripped the country, and investors large and small convinced themselves that shares in the new technology companies, the railways, would grow in profit for ever. Many of the railway companies, however, were poorly run, or had been created to build lines for which there was no commercial justification. Finally common sense prevailed, the bottom dropped out of the market, and thousands of pounds were wiped off share prices almost overnight. Many companies went to the wall and many investors were bankrupted.*

*Already, in 1844, the Government felt forced to intervene in the running of the railway network, recognising that control of the country's main transportation system could not be left in private hands. Companies were required to run at least one train a day on which the fares were capped at one penny a mile, and the Government reserved the right to take railways under public control if they failed to deliver a service. After 1847 investment continued at a lower level, but now public interest as well as shareholder profit was the motivation.*